## DATE DUE

P9-CCS-714

"To be a s[...]ess you need to in[...]ence others, communicate persuasively, and win the hearts and minds of those around you. Dianna Booher can give you the expert advice you need to succeed."

> —Darren Hardy, publisher and editor of *Success* magazine and *New York Times* bestselling author of *The Compound Effect*

"Dianna Booher may have accomplished the impossible. By following the tactics revealed in *What More Can I Say?*, you will communicate in a way that creates a dynamic engagement with others after which all parties walk away satisfied and smiling. Excellent work from one of today's most important communication experts."

> —Marshall Goldsmith, author or editor of 34 books, including the global bestsellers *Mojo* and *What Got You Here Won't Get You There*

"Booher's *What More Can I Say?* does say it all in a way that's relevant, specific, compelling, and credible."

> —Ralph D. Heath, former executive vice president of Lockheed Martin Aeronautics Company

"This is a wonderful book, fast-moving and enjoyable, loaded with practical ideas to make you a more influential and powerful communicator."

> —Brian Tracy, author of *The Power of Charm*

"Dianna Booher has done it again! *What More Can I Say* is the definitive book on the hows and whys of communicating effectively. I've always said leadership is an influence process—and to influence others, you have to know how to get your point across clearly. What more can I say, other than 'Read this brilliant book!'"

> —Ken Blanchard, coauthor of *The One Minute Manager* and *Legendary Service*

HF
5718
.B6544
2015

# WHAT MORE CAN I SAY?

---

## WHY COMMUNICATION FAILS
## AND WHAT TO DO ABOUT IT

---

Dianna Booher

PRENTICE HALL PRESS

KVCC KALAMAZOO VALLEY
COMMUNITY COLLEGE
LIBRARY

**PRENTICE HALL PRESS**
**Published by the Penguin Group**
**Penguin Group (USA) LLC**
**375 Hudson Street, New York, New York 10014**

USA • Canada • UK • Ireland • Australia • New Zealand • India • South Africa • China

penguin.com

A Penguin Random House Company

WHAT MORE CAN I SAY?

Copyright © 2015 by Dianna Booher
Penguin supports copyright. Copyright fuels creativity, encourages diverse voices,
promotes free speech, and creates a vibrant culture. Thank you for buying an authorized
edition of this book and for complying with copyright laws by not reproducing, scanning,
or distributing any part of it in any form without permission. You are supporting writers
and allowing Penguin to continue to publish books for every reader.

Prentice Hall Press is a registered trademark of Penguin Group (USA) LLC.

ISBN: 978-0-7352-0533-8

An application to catalog this book has been submitted to the Library of Congress.

First edition: January 2015

PRINTED IN THE UNITED STATES OF AMERICA

10  9  8  7  6  5  4  3  2  1

*Text design by Tiffany Estreicher*

While the author has made every effort to provide accurate telephone numbers, Internet addresses,
and other contact information at the time of publication, neither the publisher nor the author assumes any
responsibility for errors, or for changes that occur after publication. Further, the publisher does not have any
control over and does not assume any responsibility for author or third-party websites or their content.

Most Prentice Hall Press books are available at special quantity discounts for bulk purchases for
sales promotions, premiums, fund-raising, or educational use. Special books, or book excerpts,
can also be created to fit specific needs. For details, write: Special.Markets@us.penguingroup.com.

COMMUNITY COLLEGE
LIBRARY

# Contents

# It's Not What You Think

You can change your world by changing your words. . . .
Remember, death and life are in the power of the tongue.

**—Joel Osteen**

Phil's name sounded vaguely familiar. A quick Internet search confirmed the connection: Our paths had crossed about twenty years earlier at a client organization. His interview for my company's general manager position ended up more like a college reunion. We reminisced about mutual friends in the business, swapped client names, and bemoaned travel mishaps.

"So why do you want to go to work for me?" I ask him. "Your LinkedIn page says you're vice president of marketing for some company."

"That's only part-time right now. The new company I'm with is just a little ahead of the market. I need something else to bridge that gap before they can afford to hire me full-time."

"Tell me about the new business, then."

His eyes light up like a Christmas tree, and he launches into an explanation about the new venture. He's working for a Hollywood movie producer, who has a few sideline businesses of play-on-demand movies in hotel chains. They produce 3-D programming sold to networks such as ESPN, Hallmark, and Disney.

"Got any reality TV shows in mind?" he asks offhandedly as he ends his tale.

"As a matter of fact, I do." I toss out a concept that had occurred to me while writing my last book.

"Hmmm. That could work. Seriously. I'll pass the idea on to Barry if you want me to. He's in LA this week. Have you been to Universal Studios? Amazing place. Anyway. Barry makes all those show decisions. I don't get into that. I just sell the programming into the hotels once the shows are shot. Occasionally, I go on one of the funding meetings—if they're close by. Like a couple of weeks ago. Barry got a few doctors in a room. Pitched them on a new series he's doing. Twenty-five minutes. They all invested $50,000, and that was enough to put the first series in the can. . . . But it's unusual for me to go."

We talk a little further about the general manager's job. But I quickly decide it's a no-go. He's a nice guy, but I need a long-termer in the position.

A week later Phil calls again. "Barry will be back from LA tomorrow afternoon. I mentioned your reality TV show to him. He wants to talk to you. Can you meet with him tomorrow at two?"

"Sure." Actually, I hadn't given the idea another minute's thought since Phil had left my office a week earlier. But I spend the rest of the day and evening writing up a treatment.

The next day Barry, Phil, and I meet in my office. We trade background information. Barry tells me about the movies he and his business partner have produced—a long string of titles that I recognize immediately. Then he overviews several reality TV shows they are currently shooting.

At this point, I decide to show him the two-page concept that I'd drafted.

He skims it, then looks up. "I like it."

"So you would be expecting me to *invest* in this show?"

"No. That's *my* job—to raise the funding. We would own the show together and split the net profits fifty-fifty."

My first thought: Maybe he's taking money out of the proceeds, so that there *is* no profit. "Could you forward a typical production budget for my review?" His assistant does so the next day.

Over the next few weeks, we meet several times to discuss the specifics of the deal. On one occasion, he brings his son with him, who is working on a documentary for the History Channel.

Barry agrees to add every clause and safeguard I propose into our written contract. He reports that a couple of networks have already expressed interest in my concept, and he has an investor for our first $60,000.

"So when are we going to start shooting the pilot?" I ask.

"As soon as I finish up the series I'm on—end of December."

December comes and goes. "So are you ready to schedule the pilot? I need to line up the talent. They travel frequently, so I need to nail down dates with them."

"We have to have at least $50- to $60,000 to shoot the sizzle reel and pilot." He explains where he thinks he can cut $10,000 out of the budget by using a simpler set and a local crew.

Budget-conscious. I like that.

Joe, Barry's show runner, calls me from Hollywood to begin discussing details: run time, music, on-camera talent, potential product placements, website, and so forth.

"So don't we have funding already committed—at least for the pilot?" I ask the next time Barry stops by the office. "I thought you said an investor had already committed $60,000?"

"He backed out." Long pause, then, "But I'm still committed to the idea. We'll get it done. We just need $50- to $60,000 to get started.

"Look, no need to be disappointed. We're busy now anyway. I'm shooting two other projects. There's no hurry with me. Unless you're in a hurry?"

"It's just that Joe has already asked me to schedule the talent, and the three contestants can be available to record this month—but I don't know about later."

"Then, look, my company will put up half of the $50,000 if you will put up the other half," Barry offers.

"Well, I didn't plan to invest any money in this myself."

"I understand. That's completely your choice. We'll just keep working on getting investors as we'd planned, then. And if you know of friends or colleagues who might like to invest, let me know. Whatever you're comfortable with."

I do more checking on Barry. One of his companies appears to have a contract with a pro sports team. The other company's website is announcing the new forthcoming 3-D series programming, featuring a legendary sports figure as its star. Two more series are listed as "forthcoming."

I write out the $25,000 check and phone him. He promises to stop by and pick it up on his next visit by the end of the week.

Joe in LA becomes the point man. I get a text message at nine a.m. "Late night. Will call you later today." No call. Next day an email would come in at eight p.m. "Sorry. Got held up in a long script meeting. Will call Thursday." On Thursday: "Have the flu. Think I'm going to rest over the weekend. Let's talk on Monday." On Monday: "No point in talking without the producer, and his current job is running over a couple of days. I'll try to set up a conference call after he's finished with this client." Next, Joe has a bad auto accident.

You know the end of this story: Barry disappeared. Phil protested innocence, and then stopped returning calls—from me or my attorney. Joe's two-line "obituary" appeared in the *Los Angeles Times* a few weeks later.

By nature, I'm a skeptical soul. So why begin this book by telling this tale of getting scammed? My point: Building trust and persuading people to do something can be quite easy if you know what you're doing.

That's both good and bad. It's good if you have a person or group's best interest at heart. It's bad if you have selfish or sinister motives in mind.

Good communicators influence people in subtle ways. They find common ground, build rapport over a long period of time, and strive to appear trustworthy. They never act like the stereotypical aggressive con artist you see in the sitcoms.

(For an analysis of all the steps Barry and Phil took to win my trust—and the trust of many others, as I later discovered from articles on the Internet about prior convictions and prison time—see the next chapter on trust.)

The more popular word of the past few years has been *influence*. But whatever term you prefer, communication is essentially about making things happen, getting action, changing behavior, or changing minds. Changing someone's mind from negative to neutral about you, a cause, or an issue may be the biggest shift of all.

In short, communicating, especially at work, is purposeful. Sure, you also communicate to inform or educate—but usually the result of that informative message or education is to influence someone to *do* something or *change* something.

The same is true in your personal life—but with an additional purpose. At home, you communicate to change relationships—strengthen them, deepen them, move them off dead center, test them, improve them, enrich them, or end them.

Yet people communicate every day to make things happen or to get a point across. They say they want to:

- *"sell* an idea"
- *"increase* their impact"
- *"recruit* top talent to come to work for their organization"
- *"educate* consumers about the advantages of their products"
- *"sway* members to support their position"
- *"urge* employees to cooperate with the new policy"
- *"inspire* others to peak performance"
- *"encourage* people to donate generously"

However they phrase it, their goal is to persuade or influence. In fact, some people hesitate to use the word *persuade* because it has taken on an almost pejorative meaning—the motif of manipulator from the movies. *Persuading* is not a dirty word. It's not about manipulation. It's a neutral word. Whether it's good or bad depends on intellectual honesty, choice, purpose, and outcome.

**Intellectual honesty:** Is it misleading or deceptive?

**Choice:** Do people have real choices about complying?

**Purpose:** Is it harmful? In whose best interest is it?

**Outcome:** What is the effect of the choice, decision, or change?

Most people equate communicating persuasively with *talking* someone into doing something. But *talking* is just a small step in the process—or may not be a part of the process at all.

Persuading is primarily about *thinking*. Talking is *one way* to communicate some of your thinking or *one way* to find how other people think, so that you know how to approach them to change their thinking.

> Persuading is primarily about *thinking.*

## The Big Challenge

Are most people eager to be persuaded, moved to action, or changed?

Empirical evidence says no. The vast majority of people (88 percent) report that they break their New Year's resolution before the end of January.[1] And New Year's resolutions are usually changes people decide they want to make themselves! So, clearly, whether they're talking about getting physically fit, financially fit, or mentally fit, people do not find change easy.

People openly resist being persuaded. They record their favorite TV programs in order to fast-forward through commercials. When the sales associate in the store says, "May I help you?" they automatically say, "No, I'm just looking"—even if two minutes later they ask for help to find something.

My point—and the challenge: People have become overburdened

with information, are skeptical of spin, and are wary of those trying to persuade them to do anything.

At the same time, more and more people are trying to break through with a message. We want to influence others to do something. Those who earn a living in sales remain a steady and significant part of the workforce—manufacturers reps, Realtors, social media marketers, pharmaceutical sales reps, financial advisors, and consultants.

And of course if you're in a service business (entrepreneurs, IT consultants, attorneys, accountants, dentists, freelance writers), you've always depended on selling skills to make a success of the venture. Influencing others to hire, sign a contract, or make a decision on the next project proves crucial to your success.

Good communication may not make a risky project sound safe, but poor communication may fail to convey the benefits of a good project or good deal.

## We're All in the Fishbowl

Another reason for your communication to be intentionally persuasive is this: You will succeed or fail in a very public way. It seems as though everybody has become a publisher! Even my eighty-nine-year-old mom is on Facebook. The masses have gained access to the Internet. After all, what else can you do with people on the other side of the globe that's fun, free, and fast except blast out your thoughts on everything from world peace to weight loss? Posts on Facebook, LinkedIn, Twitter, Google+, and blogs have become as much a daily habit as eating. Smartphones seem to be an extension of the human hand. Text messages can be received instantaneously around the world.

The self-publishing phenomenon blasts out even more persuasive messages: e-books, white papers, reports, webinars, videos on YouTube and Vimeo. Everywhere you turn, people are screaming at you to pay attention to their ideas: Do this, don't do that, buy this, attend that, believe that, adopt this strategy, discover the secret to X. They either love your ideas—or hate them. They either affirm you and your approaches or debunk them—loudly and publicly.

So, from CEO to entry-level employee, from soccer parent to retired golfer, we all live in a fishbowl now. A hallway conversation can be captured on someone's cell phone, posted online, and go viral in a matter of seconds, and as a result, careers and earnings take a nosedive. CEOs can't hide in the corner office with an assistant to shelter them from the world. Teachers no longer rule their classroom when students can flip out their cell phones and push the Record button. Employees can no longer claim innocence when a colleague whistleblower can tweet evidence.

Once words leave your mouth, credibility goes either up or down. Trust remains stable, grows, or plunges.

All the raw ingredients of communication (words, body language, emotion, logic, action, inaction, listening, branding, perception, structure, and so forth) produce change—either positive or negative.

## The Nine Core Principles of Persuasive Communication

This book presents nine core principles of persuasive communication. As we move through each chapter, you'll see what causes communication to fail and what makes communication succeed in changing behavior or changing minds:

The Law of Trust vs. Distrust

The Law of Collaboration vs. Monologue

The Law of Simplicity vs. Complexity

The Law of Tact vs. Insensitivity

The Law of Potential vs. Achievement

The Law of Distinction vs. Dilution

The Law of Specificity vs. Generalization

The Law of Emotion vs. Logic

The Law of Perspective vs. Distortion

I'll examine each of these core principles and explain how to apply them practically so that you can use them immediately to get your point across, bring about change, inspire others to take action, encourage your family member or team, or sell a product or service more successfully.

That's our mission in the following pages.

—Dianna Booher

# 1

---

# The Law of Trust
# vs. Distrust

The most important persuasion tool you have in your entire
arsenal is integrity.                                    **—Zig Ziglar**

Trust is the glue of life. It's the most essential ingredient in
effective communication. It's the foundational principle that
holds all relationships.                            **—Stephen Covey**

Trust is built with consistency.                  **—Lincoln Chafee**

So what are your responsibilities here?" I asked Cheryl Barruso,
the senior manager seated beside me at the back of the room
during the leadership meeting.

"Actually, I haven't figured all of them out yet. They just created
a new position for me. We're realigning things now. I've only been
here a few weeks."

"You've intrigued me." I paused, undecided whether I knew this
client well enough to pry. "So what do you say to top officials to

persuade them to create a new position for you? What's your key area of expertise?"

She looked at me with a most passionate gleam in her eye: "I can lead a team of hundreds through a monumental change initiative, where they follow me blindly over the edge of a cliff. We'll parachute down to a whole new world and deliver the desired outcome on time and within budget—and they'll love me, not hate me, at the end of the journey!"

I could tell she'd said it dozens of times, after days of thought.

Cheryl's secret to gaining such trust? "It is my ability to communicate and connect with people. . . . When your team feels a real connection with you, they'll view you as an integral part of the team. They never look at you as though you're merely shouting plays from the sidelines."

Of course, Cheryl didn't come to the conclusion and identify that expertise so easily and quickly. But that's not my point here—persuasion, trust, and results are. And they are intricately linked.

Ever worked for a boss who had a habit of pointing out others' mistakes publicly in a staff meeting? Chances are good that when the boss later asks for feedback on an idea, the group remains silent.

Maybe you've been disappointed by a colleague's lack of follow-through on promises. A client asks you and your teammate for a proposal to be delivered on Friday. Since you have most of the information at hand, you volunteer to draft the lengthy proposal—all except the customized pricing component. Your teammate offers to have the pricing ready to insert the day before your meeting. When the time comes, he says he still lacks one number, but will be ready to insert the one page by eight the next morning, before your eleven o'clock client meeting. The next morning, he gets the page to you at ten thirty. You insert it, make copies, and dash out the door to the client's office without adequate time to review the pricing. And the client has questions about the pricing that you can't answer.

In both of these situations, trust has been destroyed. And those who lose trust may never know the significance of what they've lost, when they lost it, why they lost it, or how to regain it.

But the loss is huge.

## Some Crooks Are Such Nice Guys!

Let's go back to the introduction. Why was Barry so successful in lifting $25,000 from my checking account when so many others fail at earning trust? Barry was able to tap into three elements that generate trust: commonality, social proof, and reciprocity.

**Commonality:** We trust people who we think are like us.

**Social proof:** We want evidence that others trust in the person, organization, or idea.

**Reciprocity:** We trust people who have our best interests at heart.

Barry transferred trust from Phil, someone with whom I had had a prior relationship. As for commonalities, Phil made it seem as though the encounter with Barry was *my* idea. Barry took time to build rapport, to discover things we had in common (children, interests, scriptwriting, friends, values, long work hours, heavy travel schedules, entrepreneurialism). He set up a collaborative work arrangement: drafting the contract, saving money in production, finding investors, planning with Joe.

As for social proof, Barry referred me to the website with client names I recognized, a contract with the pro sports team (or so the website of his sister company claimed), and a "forthcoming" TV series with a sportscaster whose name was a household word, as well as the "doctors" nearby who had each invested $50,000.

Even reciprocity came into play when he offered to contribute up to half the funding on "my" idea. What kind of fool would withhold the other half after such a generous offer?

As for another element of persuasion (scarcity), time and opportunities were short; Barry and his crews had limited time. Their production schedule was filling up fast. Projects had to fall into their queue as they got funded. According to Barry, TV networks scheduled new series only twice a year—spring and fall. They created a sense of urgency—but not around receiving my money. They increased my trust by pretending to look out for my best interest rather than theirs by *not* rushing to collect my check and pretending not to be in a rush to schedule the series—all the while letting me know that "time was running out in the marketplace." In fact, the longer we waited for funding, the more they seemed to lose interest in the idea.

Trust in any situation doesn't just happen. It develops over time, with intention. These "nice guys" had intentions!

## Can You Transfer Trust?

Sure—if you're transferring it to other people's account for *their* benefit. Survey after survey shows that people make decisions every day by asking others for opinions.[1] We check the Twitter feed to see what people are saying about new movies. We ask Facebook friends about favorite restaurants or books to buy. We read endorsements on LinkedIn for supplier recommendations. We call a friend or family member for a referral on a financial advisor.

Marketers have not missed this point about the value of personal referrals.

Investment counselors invite their clients for a complimentary dinner at a posh restaurant to sit at the same table with prospects so that they can chat about how much they trust and enjoy working with the host of the event. Mass emailers send out offers through associates with an opening paragraph or two that says:

> *Dianna,*
>
> *I thought you'd be interested in this wonderful opportunity offered by my buddy Bob—available for just the next 48 hours! Click here for the details. . . .*
>
> > *Catch you later,*
> > *James*

Never mind that you don't know anyone named James, or at least, that you don't know James all that well. The marketing technique is to simulate a personal recommendation from a friend.

For the most part, however, people don't conveniently find themselves in situations where they can *easily transfer trust from others to themselves.* As with money, they have to earn trust the hard way— over time, with intention.

Trust doesn't come easy. After all, do you trust every blog that you run across—or only a few? Do you trust information in a tweet from those you don't know? Do you believe all ads? Do you hesitate to click on attachments to strange emails that land in your in-box? Do you consider all news reports to be objective?

More and more, we trust fewer and fewer people and sources. The key question we ask about the transfer of trust: Who benefits—me or you?

## What Creates Distrust?

Headlines around the globe remind us daily about the mismanagement, moral lapses, and malaise at the top of corporations and government bureaucracies. Likewise, security leaks and terrorist threats have led to the now-familiar slogan: "If you see something, say something." While that top-of-the-mind motto may make us safer physically, it also makes us feel more vulnerable emotionally when we decide to trust.

Individuals, too, may create a sense of distrust in several ways:

- lies, dishonesty, half-truths, cover-ups, deception in all its forms
- moral lapses in all their forms (values people claim to hold do not match what they actually do)
- blaming others for failures, not accepting personal responsibility for mistakes, weaknesses
- inconsistency in actions, decisions, directions, rewards (people seem to have different standards in different circumstances)
- incompetence (people have no worthy goals or mission except self-interest)

These people rarely recognize themselves. Often, they're the same people bemoaning the lack of respect and trust from others.

## Build Trust, and They Will Respond

As I interviewed executive after executive about the most important thing leaders can do to build trust, they agreed on the most crucial principles:

### Tell the Truth

How many times have you heard or read this line after a senior official is kicked out of the job: "He's leaving to pursue other interests" or "She's leaving to spend more time with her family"? Automatically, you roll your eyes, "Right." Then within a few hours, days, or weeks, the rest of the story unfolds: the scandal, the fraud, the earnings report.

Groupon, the deal-of-the-day website that features discounted gift certificates usable at local or national companies in markets around the world, generated a different discussion: Its CEO Andrew Mason got attention when he sent out this announcement to his employees in 2013: "After 4½ intense and wonderful years as CEO of Groupon, I've decided that I'd like to spend more time with my family. Just kidding—I was fired today." He went on to detail why: the company's drop in performance.

Although everyone might not applaud the company's performance at the time of his departure, he certainly earns top marks for trust. Rather than the typical mumbo-jumbo about leaving to "pursue other interests," he sent out an honest exit message.

His truth telling hasn't been lost on those who watch CEOs and success stories. A *Wall Street Journal* story details Mason's exit and that of David Yost, former CEO of AmerisourceBergen. After fourteen years at the helm, Yost decided that he'd had his shot and it was time for new blood and new ideas in the company. So he brought in his successor, trained him for a year, and then moved on. Results? The company's shares traded at a split- and merger-adjusted price of approximately $5 when Yost took over as CEO and traded at $41 when he left.

So did he earn or lose trust? The *Harvard Business Review* named him one of the world's "100 Best CEOs."[2]

Tell people what you know. As one executive put it, "During our merger, we even told them we had certain information and at what point in the future we would be allowed to reveal that information." Nothing earns trust like straight talk from leaders about bad news, poor performance (yours, theirs, the organization's), mergers, layoffs, mistakes, crises, plans.

## Take Them Along

Good decisions can turn into nightmares when communicated poorly. Often leaders go through all the A–Z reasoning, argue the pros and cons of an issue, walk through the entire execution of a plan in their head until they are absolutely convinced their decision is in the best interest of everyone concerned.

Then, finally convinced and committed themselves, they fail to communicate the reasoning to all the other people who have to come along with them—those who have to implement the decision.

Jane Binger, senior research officer at Sutter Health Systems, says, "I was in an organization of 60,000 people, where they planned to centralize to gain economies of scale and to rid the organization of waste. But they failed to explain the reasons for the centralization to the more than 100 entities involved.

"Instead, they sent one long email telling about how they were going to do it and talking about going to one logo for the whole organization. They actually thought people would like it and support it. Only *one* person I talked to supported the idea. All the others thought the company was *taking something away* from them. They read the message to mean, 'You are failing.' People were genuinely hurt over the logo change. Some were even tearful about the change."

To have others trust you means trusting them with your reasoning behind decisions, details, and data.

## Be Likable

Until they prove themselves to be liars, we tend to trust people we like. And we like people most like us: those who have the same interests, the same hobbies, the same values. Go to a big convention, and you'll see people link up by state or region for "meet-and-greet" socials.

Physical attractiveness helps. You don't need movie-star good looks, but what most cultures consider attractive is a symmetrical face, a proportionately sized body, clear skin, healthy hair, straight teeth.[3] We judge attractive people to be happier, smarter, nicer, more successful, more convivial, more intriguing, and of higher moral character.[4] Attractiveness even affects your wallet as well as your trust account. Researchers discovered that physically attractive real-estate agents list homes for $20,275 more and sell the homes for $15,622 more than average-looking agents.[5]

But likability is about more than being genetically blessed. Plenty of factors are within your control that will make you more appealing to people you are looking to influence. Good grooming, a pleasant facial expression, and confident body language all count. Tone of voice and word choice matter a great deal. The thoughtful gesture or word makes you approachable. Remembering and using people's names make you even more appealing.

Bob Danzig, former president at Hearst Newspapers, led a team of 6,000 employees during his twenty-year tenure. When he was traveling to one of his field offices, his executive assistant would send a memo the evening before his arrival: "Bobby will be visiting tomorrow." Notice the use of the informal "Bobby." At his direction, the next morning before he left, she'd have compiled for him a list of people at that site, along with their achievements. Bob sent a personal note to their homes, congratulating each of them on their work. He'd put an *S* or an *F* by each name on the list. Those with an *F* got flowers. Those with an *S* got either a Tiffany's bracelet or a money clip. Hearst spent about $30,000 a year on such gestures. Why? In essence, the gesture meant, "We respect you, we want to encourage you, and we trust you to do important work."

Packaging counts (grooming, facial expression, gestures, fitness). The wrapping creates intrigue, making others want to get to know the personality beneath the surface. As people come to know you, they learn to like you.

In short, pay attention to people. Find out what you have in common. Treat them with courtesy. Demonstrate respect by your body language, your dress, your grooming, your language, your tone of voice, and your habits when around them.

## Demonstrate Competence

But no matter how much you like some people, you can't trust them. In the early days of my company, I hired a designer who was talented and personable, and left the job in his hands—including a custom-design project for an important client. At various checkpoints, his oral reports boiled down to "All is well, no questions."

Just a few days before the project due date, I asked to see the finished product and discovered that almost nothing had been done. He had no idea how to complete the project; I had to take it on myself to meet the deadline. After we got past that deadline and I dug into his other activities and outcomes, I discovered chaos.

He proved to be a delightful, but totally incompetent, designer.

Where competence is concerned, one mistake can cast doubt, two mistakes can put others on notice, and three mistakes can close your trust account. Competence is a prerequisite for trusting and following a leader.

## Be Confident, Hopeful, and Optimistic

Coaches of sports teams do it. Commanders during wartime do it. Corporate leaders do it. To persuade people to do their best and keep moving ahead despite the odds, you have to instill confidence that they can achieve the goal before them.

When food-processing company Ingredion made a significant change in its business structure, they encountered concerns. "When we broke up the $1.5 billion entity, there was uncertainty among the employees involved in the merger of the two companies: 'Where will we be in two years?'" Han Kieftenbeld, global chief procurement officer of Ingredion, explains. "We wanted to be transparent in our communication with employees and create clarity about where that would be, about our strategy to grow, and about our vision."

How did they achieve that clear, positive vision for their employees?

"We didn't promise anything, but we were very convinced we could grow. The employees could see the glass as half-full or half-empty. I'm sure they were asking themselves, 'Why stay with this company?'

"So we were transparent about what things we could and couldn't say during the transition. As a result, we had very low attrition rates, and almost all felt very positive about the merger. In our industry and in a global company like ours with a large workforce in Asia, it's not uncommon to see attrition rates in the double digits. Ours was under 2 percent during this two-year period."

Optimism and confidence (and their counterparts, pessimism and uncertainty) are contagious.

## Communicate Consistently and Repeatedly

Silence breeds distrust; openness increases trust. Even unbelievably outrageous messages, unfortunately, can be persuasive if delivered often and consistently.

The Nazis proved the effectiveness of a consistent message repeatedly delivered. On a visit to Dachau concentration camp near

Munich, Germany, where more than 200,000 Jews were imprisoned and more than 41,000 were murdered between 1933 and 1945, I asked our tour guide, "How did the townspeople not know what was happening in these gas chambers so near the center of town?" The guide hung her head: "They were told over and over, 'It's just a factory. They pay incentives and taxes. It's good for the community.'"

"But didn't anyone get suspicious, go to the site, and check things out?" I asked.

She shrugged. "Yes, they did. There were official walk-throughs and inspections. But they never allowed people to see what was *really* happening on those tours. They just kept telling the same story: 'It's just a factory. They pay taxes. It's good for the town.'"

Consistent messages delivered over time gradually sink in— even if those messages are wrong, vicious, horrendous.

But consider this: When the consistent communication is uplifting, encouraging, and delivered in a culture of trust, the message is even easier to accept.

Catherine Hernandez-Blades, chief communications officer at Flextronics, talks about a strong culture of trust in a former organization, a large defense contractor: "They did a great job of building trust because of their communication processes. They had a webcast studio. The president did a monthly chat with all employees. We had an app for all managers and supervisors that pushed monthly briefings to them—charts, PowerPoints, everything they needed to use in their staff meetings to get the message out. This built enormous trust because people knew they were going to be communicated with routinely. If they had questions, they knew there was a forum where they could get answers.

"By contrast, what I find amazing is in Silicon Valley, where there are so many tools to communicate. . . . So many of these companies don't take advantage of them. They're very secretive. When you go into meetings inside the valley, it feels different. . . . The element of trust is gone. And yet it could easily be achieved through the use of their own tools!"

Secrecy breeds rumors. Regular communication, on the other hand, drives out paranoia and drives up trust.

## Make Sure Your Body Language Underscores Trust

The body language of distrust and/or dishonesty: Leaning away. Feet pointed away from the person you're talking to (as if trying to escape). Averting eyes (except in some Latin American countries, where this is a sign of respect for one's elders). Touching the mouth or nose (lying). Arms folded (closed mind, defensiveness). A forced smile, no eye involvement (insincere).

To show trust, maintain eye contact (but don't stare, of course). Use open gestures above the waist. Sit or stand in a relaxed, comfortable, but attentive posture. Smile naturally.

## Demonstrate Trust to Gain Trust

An atmosphere of trust—or its absence—is created from the top of an organization. If people feel that they must "win at any price," then that's the game they play every day they come to work—with their boss, their customers, their suppliers. If their supervisor penalizes people for mistakes, they hide them. If leaders allow freedom to take risks, fail, and try again, people thrive in doing their best to succeed.

Some common signs of trust: Providing trial products and loaners. Establishing credit approvals immediately. Trusting employees with inside news. Forgoing the signing of non-disclosures for minor discussions. Allowing overtime work and reporting hours without supervisors present.

A data-entry employee landed a new job after being unemployed for more than a year. Wide-eyed with excitement at the opportunity to make overtime money and rebuild her depleted savings, she told me, "There's a big backlog at my new company. And my boss said he's fine with me coming in to work on Saturdays to catch up and make a little overtime pay. And he's not even there! Can you believe that? I love that place! I just report my hours to them for my time on Saturday mornings. They actually trust me to do that!"

The first filter for those who influence us positively is, "Do I trust this person?" Communication fails as distrust sets in; communication succeeds as trust grows. After people trust you, they'll decide whether to consider what you have to say or what you want them to do.

Never fail the first test.

# 2

---

# The Law of Collaboration vs. Monologue

Real-time collaboration is the hot button of the future. . . . It's being built into sales force automation tools (customer relationship management) and accounting. **—Robert Mahowald**

Resilience is really about collaboration and mutual understanding. **—Roger Simpson**

A single question can be more influential than a thousand statements. **—Bo Bennett**

People don't always do what serves them best. They do what they *perceive* serves them best. Believing that you have the better—or only—grasp of reality or truth may stand in the way of influencing others.

Neither can you assume that people understand *how* to change even if you both agree on the same "truth" and the ultimate goal. An initiative to "improve the customer experience" may be totally agreeable to a customer-service agent, for example, but the "how" can be a bit mystifying. "Saving more money for college" may sound like a great goal to your spouse—but with no actual plan in mind, his spending habits will probably not change.

And leaders can't assume that people will follow through on an action—even if they *do* understand how to achieve the goal. People know how to vote, but many don't. People know how to exercise, but many don't. People know how to send in a pledge they've committed for those suffering after a tragedy or for a charitable cause, but many don't.

To influence someone to follow through on action, you have to start with the other person's reality—not yours. For example, you go to customers and make a sales presentation on a splashy, innovative product—*your* reality and *your* perception of what will serve them. But you discover they're interested in only the lowest pricing for a generic product.

> To influence someone, you have to start with the other person's reality—not ours.

Collaboration comes into play at this point. And collaboration calls for conversation.

So how well do leaders collaborate? According to research by Zenger Folkman, published at HarvardBusinessReview.org, not so well. The most common area of weakness for ineffective senior leaders is their inability to develop others on their team to perform at their highest level, followed by their inability to collaborate. But the good news is: These leaders can change these bad habits.[1]

When collaborating, choose your words carefully to make sure you do not convey that the other person's point of view is invalid. Offer nuanced statements like these:

"My understanding is that . . ."

"I hear what you're saying. My experience has been different . . ."

"The way I see it is that . . ."

"My impression of what's happening here is . . ."

"What I'm interpreting in this situation is . . ."

"From my point of view, you could . . ."

"It seems to me that . . ."

Arrogant statements like these build a wall:

"The truth of the matter is . . ."

"What it all boils down to is that you just don't . . ."

"The *reality* of the situation is that . . ."

"What's *really* going on here is . . ."

"If you really want to know the truth about all this, it's that . . ."

## Don't Make Them Duck

Let's say that your friend Spencer calls and asks if you'll be home in the next hour; he wants to stop by to show you "something." You invite him to come on over. You're guessing that he has either a new laptop or car—he's been talking about buying both.

When he arrives, he chit-chats a few minutes about nothing in particular and then pulls out his laptop—the same one he's had for a couple of years. Then he announces, "So are you ready for my big news? I've changed jobs. I'm selling security systems. So I wanted to give you a demo and see if you're interested?"

At this point, would a little protective screen drop down between you? Oops, here comes a sales pitch. How do I get out of this situation?

My guess is that you'd try to keep the two-way *conversation* going as it had been before he pulled out the laptop: "I didn't know you'd changed jobs—how did you find it? How's the commute? How do you like working there?" And my guess is that Spencer would answer your questions quickly and then try to refocus on the one-directional pitch, telling you about his product.

Pitching—whether a formal sales pitch, an elevator pitch, or a crafted commercial—causes people to duck. A conversation, on the other hand, invites them to engage and exchange information. If you intend to persuade, make sure you're conversing, not pitching. Keep the discussion two directional.

## Give Ownership

Collaborating to influence has become a fundamental leadership skill. On every front, leaders put forth "draft" ideas and then ask, "What am I missing?" "Where are the fatal flaws?" "What kind of push-back will we get on this?" They expect the ideas to come pouring in from their staff.

Han Kieftenbeld says it like this: "If your objective is to get something done—versus get credit for it—you have to have collaboration. You yourself may be clear about what you want to get done. But your team hasn't come through the thought process as you have.

So you have to present your ideas as a work in progress. Then leave yourself some wiggle room. Some people may think many of the ideas are their own. That's good. They will add ideas. The concept should not come across as already cooked, baked, done."

From Hollywood screenplays to Main Street boardrooms, collaboration separates the winners from the losers. Kimberly D. Elsbach, writing in the *Harvard Business Review*, published research she gathered over six years of observing pitch meetings to Hollywood producers as well as corporate executives. After sitting in product design, marketing, and venture-capital sessions and conducting interviews with the executives responsible for evaluating the new ideas, she identified three primary categories for professionals who pitch (along with Hollywood labels):

**Show Runners** (smooth and professional): Defined as having a combination of creativity, passion, wit, charm, technical know-how, and practical thinking (including marketing savvy and financial constraints), they seek to collaborate on ideas they pitch.

**Artists** (quirky and unpolished): Defined as nonconformist in dress and mannerism, often socially awkward, with little or no interest in implementing their ideas, they try to enthrall with their concept itself.

**Neophytes** (inexperienced and naive): Defined as eager learners, unencumbered by tradition, they plead ignorance and display bold confidence and enthusiasm, which "catchers" often find enticing.

Overwhelmingly, the most successful at pitching ideas, according to the research, were the show runners. The "catchers" of the pitches attributed their success to the show runners' willingness to collaborate. They toss out an idea, level the playing field, and engage the "catchers" to make the idea their own.[2]

Successful corporate leaders understand the idea of collaboration to launch new ideas or reshape thinking.

Consultants use the same collaborative approach for the same reasons: to give ownership and get the best ideas. When I go into client organizations to improve the effectiveness of their sales presentations or proposals or increase their productivity with written communication, I start with questions—not answers. Of course, because my organization has been consulting for more than three decades, it would be far quicker and easier to start with "Here's what works . . ."

But for clients to take responsibility for the outcome, they need to share the process of building the idea.

If you have kids, you understand this concept. You pay for the toys, the clothes, or the car, and your kids fail to take care of them. They lose them, leave them out in the hailstorm, or lend them to a careless friend. But when your children buy the toy, clothes, or car out of their own hard-earned cash, they safeguard them, protect them, and pay attention to who touches them.

The principle that "people value what they create" applies to ideas as well as to items.

The principle that "people value what they create" applies to ideas as well as to items.

## Clarify the Pain or Impact

"How can we improve our steaks?" came up several years ago as an internal discussion at Brinker International, the parent company of several highly popular restaurant chains across North and South America, Asia, Africa, and the Middle East. David Parsley, senior vice president of supply chain management, who joined the organization only two years earlier, decided to try what he called the "triad approach" to collaboration.

The company brought three groups of people into the same room to talk about the product in a "steak summit": a food scientist, a chef (from the culinary team), and a commodity specialist (from the procurement/supply management team). Then, quarterly, they invited suppliers for a day to discuss how the quality was performing. His challenge at the end of these meetings: Come back to us with your best ideas on how to continue to improve quality, increase customer satisfaction, adjust our menu mix, and lower costs. Result: collaborative efforts that have been a huge success for Brinker and its brands.

In short, this Brinker example well illustrates collaborating to develop impact. Senior Vice President Parsley brought his team together to envision what the impact could be with input from the three areas of expertise.

However, sometimes you, as an individual or organization, can't envision or contribute to a solution. You can only lead people to feel the pain—that is, you ask questions and collaborate so that others feel the impact of *not* changing their approach to a particular issue.

For example, my company might lead an engineering client to consider the impact of poor writing with these questions: How much time does your average engineer spend writing reports? How many hours per week are spent writing emails? So that totals $x$ hours per week—or roughly 50 percent of the engineer's time spent writing, correct? If you ask for a rewrite on half of those reports, how much do you estimate that salary cost to be?

So much for collaborating on the pain of unchanged behavior. You can also collaborate on the impact of future change with this discussion: You mentioned that you lost the XYZ contract because your team delivered a lousy sales presentation—according to your prospect. What was the value of that contract? What's your current closing ratio once you get to the "top three" list in your sales cycle? What percentage of the time does feedback suggest that you lost a deal based on the sales presentation alone? If your sales team could increase its closing ratio by just 10 percent within the next thirty days, what would that mean in revenue in the next quarter?

Questions allow the other person to collaborate on the data you're collecting. That done, people find it difficult to invalidate their own data when you use it to ask them to consider a change.

But people still may not *do* anything about pain until it becomes urgent, even excruciating. The pain must push them past the "take two aspirin and get a good night's rest" stage to the point they're ready to head for the ER. Likewise, you'll find it difficult to persuade people to change or correct "small" problems. They may correct only "big problems." They don't lose that extra weight until their twenty-year class reunion invitation arrives or until they hit the magic number that is "too much." They don't do a proposal writing course until they lose a $200 million contract or their biggest client. The sports league doesn't adopt a zero-tolerance policy against hazing until they're slapped with a criminal-negligence lawsuit.

At some point, the pain panic button will go off. When it does, you can lead them forward.

## Engage Them With Gadgets

Many organizations build their websites with engagement in mind. Financial planners have online tools to help you budget for your first home, project your taxes, or live well in retirement. Consulting firms offer assessments to intrigue prospects on self-improvement topics. Health-care sites provide quizzes for people to compare symptoms to diagnose and determine whether they need to see a doctor.

Such tools pull people toward greater engagement—usually investigating products and services offered by the individual or organization. These products and services introduce change. It's a step-by-step approach: engage, educate, change.

If you're face-to-face with someone you want to influence, the principle still applies. Have your listener actually do something—handle a demo, write something, circle something on a brochure for later reference, walk with you to see something, hold something for you, move their chair closer to your laptop, click the link on your tablet to see a video clip. Any such action compels them to engage with your message at the moment.

## Lead Them to Reciprocate

The principle of reciprocity also works as a collaborative method to nudge people to consider your viewpoint or the action you're advocating. The origin of this idea is as old as the saying, "If you scratch my back, I'll scratch yours," which likely originated in the English navy back in the seventeenth century.

You walk through the supermarket, and a smiling woman hands you a sample sausage, cracker, or cookie. "What—you don't like that flavor? Well, here—try another flavor." She hands you the second cookie.

You don't particularly like that, either. "Okay, here's another. I know you'll love this kind—it's my favorite. And here's a one-dollar coupon to try a package."

After you've sampled three free cookies and engaged in several minutes of conversation, it's doubtful you're just going to walk away. You're more likely to pick up a bag and toss it in your cart.

But actually it takes much less than that for the principle of reciprocation to kick in. According to various studies, people feel obligated to buy after being given as little as a complimentary bottle of water.[3] Notice how the upscale department stores offer shoppers complimentary sodas as they browse. Or how about a simple gesture of kindness or a friendly word in a sea of rudeness? Yes, the research says that that, too, nudges you to buy. Consider what a wine-and-cheese party at a fashion show can do for revenue.

## Turn Their Statements Into Questions

Be known for the questions you ask—not for the answers you give. Questions serve four primary roles in collaboration and persuasion. Statements imply that you have all the answers and will control the interaction. Questions imply that the other person's input has value and can alter the discussion so that you arrive at a mutually agreeable decision or action.

As a first step, questions bring to the surface all kinds of information you will need to know in order to change someone's thinking or behavior: Where do they stand on an issue? What's important to them? What are their goals? Timelines? Limits? Who's important to them? Who influences them? How do they process information? What do their word choices tell you—are they primarily visual, verbal, or conceptual in processing information?

A second reason to ask questions is to discover roadblocks and resistance to change. Melissa, an employee at a large manufacturing organization, grew more and more frustrated as she tried to present ideas to her boss. Always well prepared with an overview of a recommendation, three to four reasons to support the recommendation, and all the research to support the concept, she routinely failed to earn approval. As she tells it, she just "never seemed to be on the boss's wavelength."

But then she started to note the questions her boss always asked about her proposed projects: "How will your recommendation advance *my* initiatives for the year? How will your project advance *my* career? Who are the *players* involved in this proposed project? Are these players central to *my* career?"

Melissa learned to frame her projects around answers to these questions: "Here's how my project fits into *your* initiative and will further *your* career. These key *players* will be involved in these ways. . . ." Then she filled in the details about the goals and outcomes of her project. Bingo. Her projects got approved.

Melissa became persuasive because she asked herself the right questions to uncover the roadblocks and then answered them in her presentations.

Questions are also used to lead to the conclusion, insight, or action you want. Members of the media master this technique early. Their degree of mastery typically determines whether they end up in prime time or relegated to the low-visibility broadcast hours. When a corporate spokesperson shows up prepared with three talking points and training in how to stay on message, her adversary, the TV anchor, determines to lead her to leak a secret, confess a liability, slam a competitor, or predict something that will make her look foolish in the morning. That's the interviewer's job.

I recently overheard a mother using a series of questions to lead her sixteen-year-old to trade in an older-model sports car for a newer sedan, not quite the model the teen had in mind: What kind of gas mileage do you get in the sports car? What kind of mileage does the Kelley Blue Book estimate for the sedan? So, at the current price of gas, how much would you save on gas per year with the newer car? If you sold your used sports car and invested that money until graduation, plus the gas money you'd save between now and graduation, how much money would you have to buy a brand-new car for college?

The teen opted to save for the newer car at graduation. Asking leading questions did the job.

A final reason to ask questions: to soften commands. When you push for agreement, the other person typically pushes back. But phrase your suggestion as a question, and the more palatable form is easier to swallow: "Would you vote to keep the doors of this school open on May 1?" Or: "May I suggest that you consider contributing more than the usual twenty-five dollars to the club this year? Here's how they're planning to use the funds. . . ."

With the question format, you've asked for permission to suggest that your listeners stop and think. They typically do.

The most powerful questions come from the person you need to persuade. For example, your prospective buyer says to you, "I like this approach." You then ask: "What appeals to you about this approach?" With her answer, you'll have valuable information.

The two-way conversation itself engages and energizes.

## Reflect: Mirror, Mirror on the Wall

For years, research studies have confirmed the power of reflecting someone's body language and speaking patterns to connect with them and build rapport.[4] In fact, the FBI and other members of law enforcement use mirroring in their interviewing process to gain information from clients.[5] Restaurant staff found this research to have a significant financial payoff. Tipping improves as the attendants match gestures, get on the same eye level as patrons, or add a friendly touch on the arm or back.[6]

To understand the power of this phenomenon, you have only to walk into a room where everybody is silent. Automatically, you'll stop talking. Enter a library or quiet museum where people speak in low whispers, and you, too, will lower your voice to a whisper. Watch others yawn, and after a few moments, you'll start to yawn. These subconscious reactions to body language around us demonstrate mirroring.

Take this mirroring further to get "in sync" with others and match their body language. If they lean forward as you talk, lean forward. If they stand and pace around in the room, stand and walk as you talk. If they speak slowly and use lots of clichés as they speak, slow your speaking rate and sprinkle in clichés.

Make your mirroring subtle. Otherwise, they'll feel mocked. And be careful that you don't work so hard to match their body language and speaking patterns that you forget to pay attention to what they're actually saying.

What's the payoff? Rapport, connection, trust—exactly what you need to influence people to change their mind or behavior.

## Empathize to Humanize

Medical research alone supports the case for empathy.[7] Doctors, health-care workers, and hospital administrators who show empathy, demonstrate concern, and apologize when things go wrong see their malpractice lawsuits decrease and their patient satisfaction scores increase.[8]

A major study led by researchers from Thomas Jefferson University and Italy to assess the relationship between physician empathy and clinical outcomes among 20,961 diabetic patients found a direct link. The higher the doctor's empathy score, the better the patients' control of hemoglobin A1c and cholesterol level. There were other correlations as well. The higher the empathy scores, the lower rate of patients with acute metabolic complications and hospital readmissions. Doctors with lower empathy scores had a 30 percent increase in hospital readmissions![9]

Empathy defuses anger and cements relationships—a first step before you can move anyone from a negative opinion to even a neutral opinion.

Once an empathetic attitude develops, its effects are easy to spot in boss-staff relationships, in doctor-patient relationships, and in customer-service interactions. Empathy comes across in a warm greeting, in a word choice, in a tone of voice, in quick action to correct a problem, in willingness to spend time with someone, or in the initiative to "go the extra mile" for someone's benefit.

Notice that most demonstrations of empathy prove impossible without true collaboration from other people about what *they* actually want, need, and value—as opposed to what *you think* they might want, need, and value.

You may have heard the old saying "No good deed goes unpunished." That may often be the sad case when someone tries to do a good deed without consulting with others to discover what they truly want, need, or value as "the good deed."

## Reframe Their Frame

Occasionally your task may be to change the entire way a person views his or her situation. Years ago, my husband and I decided to move to another nearby suburb, so we linked up with a Realtor to sell our house on Overlake Court. We had plenty of time to sell, so we set the price at the top end of the range.

"It's a buyer's market," our Realtor advised after a few months when we'd had only a few lookers. "You've overbuilt for the neighborhood. You have the largest house in the area. I think you're going to have to lower the price."

I said, "But we're counting on that price as equity in the new house we're building."

"I understand," she said. "Let me give it some thought. I have an idea. I'll get back to you."

After a couple of weeks she came back to us with this approach. "Have you thought about donating your house?"

My jaw dropped. Had she lost her mind? Had she not heard us?

She repeated the question: "Have you thought about donating your house in exchange for a charitable tax donation to be taken over the next few years? Obviously, you wouldn't get the sales price up front. But—depending on your tax situation—such an arrangement may mean more to you in deductions over the next few years than you would net from the sale if you sold it right now at your asking price. If you'd like to consider that, I can explain how that works in more detail."

We nodded, and she went on to explain the law by which nonprofits such as orphanages and hospitals are eligible for matching funds when they receive such donations from private citizens.

The bottom line: We donated our house to a local nonprofit and got a charitable deduction on our taxes for the next several years. The nonprofit benefitted by being able to double their money through the matching funds. The buyer of the house benefitted by getting a great house at a bargain price. We benefitted by getting the equivalent of our selling price in tax savings over the next few years.

This creative Realtor totally reframed our situation from "How do we price this house to sell?" to "How do we get the money we need from this house?" By doing so, by collaborating with and bringing together all the parties who stood to benefit, by reframing the situation to us as a question, she encouraged us to think more creatively. Had she simply approached us with a "Here's how to do it" plan, we would never have investigated the idea—and, frankly, would have considered her a little too inexperienced to tackle such a challenge.

As I coach executives to meet the media or engage with their largest clients, reframing remains an ongoing challenge. Here's an example of reframing in that context:

**Question** *(from a shareholder challenging "excessive" travel costs)*: "In looking at last year's costs, it seems that international travel has been extensive by anybody's criteria. How do you decide what's a worthwhile trip and what is not?"

**Reframing Response:** "We look for business-development opportunities based on these categories: The biggest bang for our buck will be linking up with strategic partners. We hope to have international partners representing us in at least six regions within the next two years.

"Another type of opportunity we're looking for is the large-conference venue, where we can place a speaker on the platform in front of 3,000 or more attendees to a meeting in our industry. And of course, we're always glad to travel to link up with an executive from an organization that expresses interest in doing business with us. A qualified buyer coming to us puts us way ahead in the sales cycle.

"For example, Jebraz International contacted us last April, interested in having us travel over and walk through their plant to tell them how we might automate some of their processes with our equipment.

"So basically those are our three criteria in looking for international business opportunities."

Notice how this question has been reframed from a "cost" issue to a matter of which business opportunities to accept.

You can reframe with bridging statements to refocus thinking. Or you can reframe simply by your word choice: "Service agents" are now "team members." "Cost" is now an "investment in your growth opportunities." "Deficit spending" is now "investment in the future." "Procrastination" becomes "attention to detail."

## Apply Peer Pressure

Ask most adults if they're susceptible to peer pressure, and they'd say no. But experience suggests otherwise: Peer pressure sways adults to change their minds and behavior as frequently as it sways teens.

One on one, a team member may argue with you for days about how to approach a project. But bring the entire team of ten together to collaborate on the project, and that one dissenting team member will find it much more daunting to continue to argue with his or her nine colleagues. A collaborative effort carries weight and lifts dissenters as it moves along toward decision and action.

At sporting events, do you cheer louder when seated with fans of the opposing team or your own team? When people are discussing who won the latest presidential debate, are you more likely to speak in groups where others seem to agree with you—or in groups where you are expressing the lone minority opinion? When you see a strong opinion on a social issue trending at the top on Twitter, are you quick to tweet an opposing view—or reluctant to do so?

Peer pressure does not necessarily decrease on the day teens turn twenty. Political candidates often report objective polling results in their campaigns for this very reason. The underlying message with such poll results is this: "Fifty-eight percent of the population think I'm the best candidate for the job. If you don't, something is wrong with the way you think." When they publish poll numbers on social issues, the underlying message is this: "Seventy-seven percent of the population approve of X. You're out of touch with your peers on this issue. What's wrong with you?"

Applied subtly, peer pressure forces people to reexamine their thinking, attitudes, and behavior and consider changes in ways few other methods of influence can.

*Collaboration closes the gaps on misunderstandings, realigns goals, and ensures shared value in the outcome.*

# 3

# The Law of Simplicity vs. Complexity

Simplicity is the ultimate sophistication.        **—Leonardo da Vinci**

Making the simple complicated is commonplace; making the complicated simple, awesomely simple, that's creativity.
                                        **—Charles Mingus**

You've often heard it said that "less is more." Occasionally, nothing is more. At least, that's what 42 West, the PR agency for the 20th Century Fox movie *The Book Thief* thought when they placed a two-page ad in the *New York Times* containing nothing but blank space. Well, almost nothing. In tiny text at the very bottom of the page was "www.wordsarelife.com." This URL redirected readers to the movie's official website.[1]

While the idea about the ad and URL parallels the movie plot (the protagonist steals books to share them with others during the World War II era in Germany), the concept also underscores the advantages of simplicity: It is compelling, clear, creative, and focused.

What does simplicity have to do with persuasion? If people don't understand the change you want them to make, they can't make that change. If they don't understand your information or explanation, you will have less of a chance to change their minds about that issue. If instructions are too complex, people will likely resist the effort to follow them—or fail to accomplish the task.

Simplicity and persuasion are intricately linked.

Health-care agencies and insurance companies, for example, continue to try to quantify the communication problem between physicians and their patients. Laura Landro, managing editor for the *Wall Street Journal* and also author of the paper's Informed Patient column, has gathered intriguing statistics from several sources about "missed messages":

- 18–45 percent of patients can't recall the major risks of their treatment.
- 44 percent of patients don't know the exact nature of their operation.
- 60–68 percent of patients don't read or understand information in a consent form.
- 80 percent of what doctors tell patients can't be recalled as soon as the patient leaves the office.
- 50 percent of what the patient does "recall" is inaccurate. [2]

While the research may not identify complexity as the sole cause for these communication failures, common sense clearly suggests that simplifying these technical and emotional conversations would improve understanding and recall.

Why does communication fail to persuade—whether physicians

are trying to influence patients to take their medications, do their therapy exercises, or control their cholesterol? Why can't salespeople get clients to increase next year's orders, or political parties persuade more citizens to turn out to vote?

The same roadblocks thwart all of these efforts: Too many ideas detract focus from the primary goals. Mixed messages bewilder people. Irrelevant details bury key ideas. Complex, disorganized documents discourage people from reading. Convoluted sentences require rereading and waste time.

Have you ever searched a company's website in frustration trying to find a phone number to call or an answer to a simple question? Ever spent fifteen minutes sorting through automated phone menus, trying to get to a live person to get a simple problem corrected? You may have become convinced that these organizations were hiding from their customers! All the while, organizations are actually spending more and more dollars to attract customers. Turning the complex into the simple makes moving people to action much easier.

Too many ideas detract focus from the primary goals. Mixed messages bewilder people. Irrelevant details bury key ideas. Complex, disorganized documents discourage people from reading. Convoluted sentences require rereading and waste time.

## Consider the Power of the One-Word Pitch, Slogan, or Response

An ambitious colleague of mine used to reflect on her climb toward career success with this line: "You've reached success when people refer to you by one name only." While I don't necessarily agree with that definition of success, the one-name definition certainly highlights *notoriety*: Oprah, Jay Z, Trump, Pelé, Saddam, Sting, Letterman, Gandhi, Mandela, Shaq, Madonna.

With attention spans growing shorter and shorter, being able to state your point or your pitch in a single word works well to grab mindshare. Look at the current and past book bestseller lists and blockbuster movies for titles that capture their essence in a word: *Blink, Switch, Contagion, Freakonomics, Casablanca, Megatrends, Superman, Exodus, Jaws, Titanic*.

Stowe Boyd, a business strategist and IT consultant, is credited with the idea of the TwitPitch. Having difficulty in scheduling meetings with start-ups at the Web 2.0 Expo, he posted a blog message saying he would no longer accept email proposals for meetings. Instead, he gave instructions for start-ups to pitch him via Twitter—very specifically: "Yes, one tweet, 140 characters less the eleven used for @Stoweboyd."

The idea has caught on. We now have tweet pitches to the media and tweet résumés sent to employers.[3] Authors query agents and publishers via tweets; publishers tweet authors for rights to license their books in other languages. (How successfully they do so in 140 characters is still debatable. But let's not get bogged down in tweets here.)

Consider, too, the impact of a one-word response to questions to influence thinking—either positively or negatively. For example, a reporter asks, "Will your organization file a lawsuit in this situation?"

You reply simply yes. The message to the offending competitor that will be played over and over on the airwaves the next day: that one word, "Yes." The message sent: "Watch out, competitor."

One-word answers pull people up short, slap them upside the head, and say, "Stop. Listen. Think."

The strength of a statement is often inversely proportionate to its length.

## Remember That Simple Does Not Necessarily Mean Short

Known as the father of advertising, David Ogilvy wrote in his book *Ogilvy on Advertising*: "Direct-response advertisers know that short copy doesn't sell. In split-run tests, long copy invariably outsells short copy." Copywriters tell us that as a rule of thumb, the higher the price of a product or service, the more words it takes to sell it.

But, of course, the goal of all persuasive communication is *not* to sell a product or service. You're selling ideas. You're selling your personal credibility—that you can complete a project on time, within budget. You're selling people on the idea that they need to follow safety precautions or take care of their health.

When persuading people that some project is easy, breaking it down into *more and smaller* steps makes more sense. You assume they know little or nothing about the project and provide *more* detail to make it simple. Making recommendations to your executive team without providing information on the relevant benefits would make the pending decision *more* complex rather than less so.

So making persuasive messages shorter rather than longer doesn't necessarily make them simple. Remember the difficulty President Obama got into when he abbreviated an important health-care issue to this short statement: "If you like your health-care plan, you can keep it. Period. If you like your doctors, you can keep them. Period."

Short does not necessarily equate to simple any more than long equates to complex. Clarity comes from language, structure, and relevance.

## Focus for Clarity

Simplicity leads to focus, which produces clarity of purpose.

"The secret of success is constancy of purpose," according to philosopher Benjamin Disraeli. Maybe that explains the downright obsession organizations have about the phrasing of their mission statements to unify employees around their visions:

**Walmart:** "We save people money so they can live better."

**Disney:** "To make people happy."

**Zappos:** "To provide the best customer service possible."

**JPMorgan Chase:** "We want to be the best financial services company in the world."

**Google:** "To organize the world's information and make it universally accessible and useful."

**Amazon:** "Our vision is to be earth's most customer-centric company; to build a place where people can come to find and discover anything they might want to buy online."

**GE:** "We have a relentless drive to invent things that matter: innovations that build, power, move and help cure the world. We make things that very few in the world can, but that everyone needs. This is a source of pride. To our employees and customers, it defines GE."

One executive recalls the chaos employees felt at an organization where he had formerly worked early in his career when the leadership team there gave them nineteen "key" initiatives for the year. He was in charge of not only implementing one of these key initiatives but also first selling the idea to all the franchisees around the world. What's more, his research traveling around the country for most of the year and meeting with senior leaders ended in his recommendation to do away with his own division as a duplication of effort—and that complex, massive project was just one of the nineteen initiatives he got tagged to tackle as part of the CEO's vision. Talk about motivation to lose focus!

For several years, as I listed strategic goals for my company, the list continued to grow: I had business goals, personal goals, learning goals, fitness goals, financial goals, and spiritual goals. As all the motivational gurus suggest, my written goals were specific, measurable, achievable, realistic, and time-sensitive. But, being plagued all my life with the mentality of an overachiever, I noticed one thing at the end of each year: Many of the goals were getting dumped to the next year's list. Try as I might, I just could not work on all of them at once. Now my list is whittled down to typically two or three for the year, and I usually achieve them all within that time frame.

No matter how much someone may want to do what you're asking, lack of focus can prevent the outcome you want. In my organization, I've had the opportunity to see this principle illustrated with training course updates. No matter how much persuasion, emphasis, influence, coercion—call it what you will—I used on my production staff to get courses updated, it was always a slow, slow process, due to their lack of complete focus. Interruptions from "routine" responsibilities and short-term client projects continued to thwart the updating process.

We tried a new approach: No more interruptions allowed. The course-update initiative became the focus. No longer considering the typical three-year time frame, I tagged "course updates" as the only initiative for the quarter and put all the production staff on the project, with no confusion about what their first priority should be.

Results: All courses were updated within a three-month (not three-year) period. The miraculous, never-before-accomplished happened—all because of focus.

Persuading someone to do something is only half the battle—they need to understand that it's their top priority.

## Limit Choices

Several collections of choices await the unwary on any given day:

- 6,000 daily newspapers in the world, many of which can be accessed through the Internet
- 40,000 movies from Amazon; 10,000 movies from Netflix
- 259 breakfast cereals
- more than 1 million apps in Android's Google Play store
- more than 1 million apps in Apple's iPhone store
- 140,000 diagnostic codes issued by the Centers for Medicare and Medicaid Services for health-care workers to choose from when they file your insurance claims

Remember the days when you used to go into a studio to have your photo made—the days before you turned on your cell phone and took your own picture? (For those of you under twenty-five, think of weddings, graduations, bar mitzvahs, or anniversary celebrations when the professional photographers are called in to take family portraits and capture the festivities.) If you are only allowed to shoot six poses, it takes about half an hour to select the best portrait. But if the photographer shoots twenty-four poses, you'll generally need to take them home for two weeks to make your selections. If it's a big to-do like a wedding and you have hundreds of photos, it might take a month to make your selections. The more choices you have, the more time is involved.

People value personal choice. That leads to the popular notion that the *greater* the choice, the *more* value. But two major research studies debunk this assumption.

One Columbia University study involved two groups of customers who were offered selections of jams at Draeger's Market in Menlo Park, California. The researchers observed and recorded the behavior of 754 shoppers as they test-tasted and bought (or did not buy) jam after being offered either six selections or twenty-four selections. The group that was offered the six selections actually bought more jam by a wide margin. Of the group of shoppers limited to six choices, 30 percent bought jam. Of the group of shoppers with the twenty-four selections, only 3 percent bought jam.

A second study was done with 193 social psychology students at Stanford University. When they were assigned an optional two-page essay for "extra credit," one group was given a choice of thirty topics for their essays. The control group was given a choice of six topics for their essays. The conditions by which the researchers measured "customer satisfaction and motivation" were the rate of assignment completion and the quality of the essay. Of those given the limited choice of topics, 74 percent turned in the assignment. Of those given extensive topic choices, 60 percent completed the assignment. The quality differential was also significant: Those with limited choices scored higher, while those with extensive choices scored lower.[4]

Salespeople in our client organizations talk about the same phenomenon in dealing with their own prospects. People want to know they *have* choices. But in solving their complex problems, they often seek out sales professionals, financial consultants, attorneys, and other advisors to help them *limit* their choices—to make their decisions easier.

The food industry, particularly, has discovered this. A headline in *USA Today* read, "Marketers Such as Starbucks Discover That Simple Sells."[5] After an era of ever-expanding menus, restaurants are slimming menu choices down to house specialties. Bestselling cookbooks are focusing on "gourmet" meals with fewer and fewer ingredients, to be prepared in less and less time.

Over-choice paralyzes people. While they initially feel motivated by the thought of extensive personal choice, having fewer options makes it easier for people to decide, buy, or do something.

## Pick a Point

Joe Calloway, author of *Be the Best at What Matters Most*, once delivered a keynote to a group of colleagues with his core message: "Pick a lane." He encouraged this group of entrepreneurs to stop trying to be all things to all people and focus on their core product line. Stories abound of large organizations that have had to learn that same lesson the hard way.

Before my keynotes, I typically sit in the audience to hear the CEO or another senior leader kick off the annual management meeting, sales conference, or industry meeting. Generally, that executive's purpose is to "set the tone," "emphasize the theme," or "lay out the focus" for the event. Occasionally, when they finish ten minutes or an hour later, their message may seem buried, lost, fuzzy.

One audience member recalls mixed messages from a former organization after several such meetings, updates, announcements, and emails. "Management kept giving us mixed messages: 'We need to *continue to grow* our business and make it better' versus 'We need to restructure our business; we're *losing money.*'"

Whether you're putting together a speech, planning a conversation, preparing for a media interview, placing a media story, meeting with a client, pitching a proposal to your boss, talking to an underperforming employee, or persuading parents of your soccer team to foot the bill to upgrade the soccer field, pick a point. Start there to simplify. Pick *one* point, theme, idea, action, or change you want to get across. That's your road map.

## Break Down the Barriers

Are your processes putting people into a tailspin? Convoluted governmental regulations and corporate policies have gagged people to the point that no one wants to utter a helpful word without a permission slip. Take the banking industry, for example. Here's a recent experience shared by a friend:

As a result of a divorce, Tracy was awarded ownership of the home she and her husband had shared during their marriage. With a copy of the divorce decree in her possession, she called the mortgage company to get the mortgage changed to her name. The rep told her, "I'm sorry, but we can't talk to you about that loan. It's in your husband's name only. He put the loan in his name when he refinanced it last year."

"I know," Tracy replied. "But I now own the home. I've faxed the divorce decree to your office several weeks ago, stating that I own the home and all proceeds from any escrow refunds, and will be responsible for the mortgage. I've been paying the mortgage for months—while the divorce decree became final. I'd like to get the mortgage put in my name."

She gave them the loan number and all pertinent information. The agent insisted that the paperwork had not yet come through to update the company's records; therefore, he could not discuss the loan. He also told Tracy she couldn't just assume the same mortgage; she would have to call the New Mortgages department and get a new loan at the higher current rate.

When Tracy called New Mortgages to start application for a new loan, the agent in that department said the mortgage company could not count any of her current income to qualify for the new loan. Requirements to qualify included a history of receiving child support for twelve months (even though her divorce had been settled only a month earlier) and six months of salary with the current employer (even though she had just taken a new job).

Tracy was forced to ask her mother to become a co-borrower on the mortgage in order to meet the bank's qualifications. Together she and her mother went through the New Mortgages department and reapplied for a new loan. The bank sent a letter saying that Tracy could not qualify for the reasons stated above, but that her mother, the co-borrower, was approved.

A day later, the bank calls Tracy back to say no can do. "If your mother is not going to *live* in the house herself, she can't be a co-borrower—she has to buy the house herself *alone* as an investment property."

Her mother agrees to do that. Tracy calls the mortgage company back to get information to move the process forward.

The mortgage company says, "We can't talk to you. If your mother is going to buy the house, she'll need to call us directly to move forward with the loan application. Ask her to call New Mortgages, extension XXX."

Her mother calls the mortgage company only to get this response: "We can't talk to you about this loan. Your daughter's name is on the original loan. We can talk only to her about this loan. Have her call the agent who originally handled the loan."

The mother protests about the runaround. The agent follows up with: "I can transfer you to the loan officer assigned to this loan package. Maybe he can help." She transfers the call.

The loan officer's response: "I hear your frustration, but I have no recall of this entire situation. My hands are tied. The husband's name is on the original loan. After you agree on a price and buy the house from him, then we can move forward!"

Companies that institute this kind of complexity and incompetence in their systems drive customers to insanity. Their representatives become memorable for their regulations, rigidity, and lack of communication.

Remove such barriers that block flexibility.

# Reduce the Noise

Little Leaguers learn to chatter the batter early: "Batter, batter, batter, batter, batter, batter, batter. Watch, watch, watch, watch, watch. Here it comes, here it comes, here it comes, here it comes, here it comes, here it comes. Whoa, whoa, whoa. Hey, hey, hey. Batter, batter, batter, batter, batter, batter, batter."

But that's nothing compared to the noise level with 60,000 fans in the stadium during the Olympics. If you've been at the scene, you know that you literally cannot hear your companions standing next to you, yelling at the top of their lungs.

That's the kind of escalated noise you're competing with as you're trying to get people's attention for your message. Yet rather than turn down the volume, people make the mistake of increasing the chatter and drowning out their own message!

For example, presenters display a slide and then talk while their audience is trying to digest what's on the slide. In effect, they're competing with their slides for the group's attention.

Salespeople do the same thing. They close a deal, get client agreement, and then keep talking—often raising concerns about the product or service that causes buyers to back out of the sale.

Catherine Hernandez-Blades, who has made a career in corporate communications, comments about one of the first few tasks when taking the helm at a Fortune 500 organization: "We cut 200 logos down to one. . . . Investor Relations deals with big data. They send out a twenty-page quarterly earnings report; the analysts interpret it in four paragraphs."

Employment specialists and talent placement firms insist that one of the key reasons organizations have difficulty filling advertised openings is that their ads are filled with clutter. They mention educational "requirements" that aren't really required at all, and list too many criteria rather than the essential skills and experience they want. Rather than persuading people to investigate the job, qualified people click away.[6]

Job applicants commit the same sins. They clutter their résumés with a track record of everything they've ever done rather than simplify so that their real qualifications get attention.

Senior leaders say that people tend to create the most noise when they are seeking funding for capital expenditures, investing, and acquisitions. But, they go on to add, recommenders frequently provide the wrong kind of information—just noise (see chapter 7 for relevance).

Nobody wants to be called a noisemaker, so why do some people chatter needlessly? Many reasons: Company culture. Diligence in their preparation. Enthusiasm. Distilling information is difficult if they're invested and involved in what you're doing. One executive explained it this way: "They tell about their project as if going on an African safari. They like to describe all the adventures along the way."

## Turn On Surround Sound

Influence has to do with consistency and repetition. Have you ever seen a clever ad on TV run just one time? Most viewers hear the ads so often they could lip-sync them by the end of the first week they air. If you're in sales and marketing, you've heard people preach the value of persistence by pointing out that prospects don't even recall your company name until about the sixth or seventh time they've heard the commercial.

Repetition on multiple channels of communication breaks through the protective shield that most people wear.

A large international defense contractor facing cancellation of a key contract with the government pulled out all the stops to persuade Congress to continue its project as vital to national defense. The contractor attributed its success to what it called a "surround sound" campaign: communicating on multiple channels. The contractor put out an extensive ad campaign, using local people in the ads. Then it blew up photos from the ads, made posters, and held press conferences with these same local people meeting with their senators and congressional representatives in face-to-face meetings around the country. Next, the contractor added radio campaigns featuring these same people. Then the contractor invited the editorial media to these face-to-face meetings, which forced public dialogue on the defense issues.

The message got through to Congress. Discussion of the defense issues on multiple channels halted cancellation of the national defense contract.

As one executive in the food service industry put it: "Some companies say it and move on. We don't. We put out a message. Then we pass it down through our routine management channels. Then our CEO mentions it again at our quarterly meetings—maybe with a new twist or in a different context. We consistently repeat that message."

## Drop the Doublespeak

People distrust what they don't understand. They don't have time to translate speeches and documents as Latin students did back in college days. Executives today are often forced to hire specialists (attorneys, accountants, auditors, tax specialists) to translate for them—unless the message is not worth the cost to plow through the gobbledygook.

David Ogilvy created many of advertising's most famous campaigns, including the best-known headline ever written for a car ad: "At sixty miles an hour, the loudest noise in this new Rolls-Royce comes from the electric clock."[7]

He knew a thing or two about persuasion. And his rule of thumb for communicating was, "If you're trying to persuade people to do something, or buy something, it seems to me you should use their language, the language they use every day, the language in which they think. We try to write in the vernacular."

Tom Hund, executive vice president and CFO at BNSF Railway, elaborates on the complexity of most business decisions made in the executive suite: "We look at all kinds of projects here. We spend about $4 billion here a year on capital additions. We look at all kinds of reasons for doing things: The economic case. Perhaps the risk litigation case. Maybe a strategic relationship with a customer—even though the economics up front don't justify the expenditure. So it's a series of reasons that go into the decision. . . . You have to take something that's complex, boil it down, and make it simple so that the average person can grasp it and form an opinion about it."

Much of what is written today in corporate America and by

governmental agencies is not intended to inform people. It is written to protect the organization providing the information. Take financial disclosures that accompany investments. Remove the jargon and what they say is, "This is a highly risky investment. Beware. We are not responsible. If you invest in this, you could lose every penny!"

But if they made that statement so clearly and boldly, nobody would invest. Strip the disclosures and doublespeak that accompany published pharmaceutical studies, and what they say is, "We are not sure how and why this new medicine works for some individuals. We don't know what the implications and complications may be in the future. Take it at your own risk. We are not responsible for what may happen to you." But if they made that statement so clearly and boldly, nobody would use the medicine without further testing.

Doublespeak persists as a protective shield. But gobbledygook also limits your influence in multiple ways: wasted translation time, distrust, and confusion. To expand your influence, ditch the doublespeak. Unravel the babble.

## Avoid Making the Effort Look Harder Than It Is

That's not the same as making things look easy. Promise people that change will be easy, and they will think you're incompetent, crazy, or a liar. When you're trying to influence people to make a change, they need to consider the request and make the commitment. Otherwise, you'll have a yes answer and a no on the follow-through.

That said, some things really *are* easy. Why make them unnecessarily difficult simply by the way you communicate them?

As with food presentation at a restaurant, sometimes getting others to do or change something hinges on your presentation of the effort involved.

Research by Hyunjin Song and Norbert Schwarz confirms that people's assessment of the effort required may be affected by something as seemingly insignificant as the font. In their first study, the researchers showed students the instructions for performing a short exercise and asked them to estimate the time they thought it would take to complete the regimen. With one group, they described the exercise routine with Arial font; with the second, they used *Brush* font. Students reading the exercise regimen in the complex font (*Brush*) estimated that it would take them almost twice as long to complete the exercise (8.2 minutes versus 15.1 minutes).

In Song and Schwarz's second study, people were asked to read a cake recipe and estimate how long it would take a chef to bake the cake. One group read the recipe in Arial; the other read the recipe in *Mistral*. The Arial group estimated the preparation to be 5.6 minutes, while the *Mistral* group estimated it to take 9.3 minutes.

In the third study, students were asked to rate how much skill the chef needed to prepare the cake. Those reading the recipe in the complex font (*Mistral*) estimated that the task required a higher degree of skill than did the students reading the recipe in the simple font (Arial).[8]

Whether you're creating an image for your Facebook page, writing web copy, sending email, drafting a client proposal, or soliciting gifts from donors, make the action you want look easy:

- Use a simple font.
- Make subject lines useful, specific, concrete.
- Provide informative headlines for easy scanning within a document.
- Create an eye-appealing layout.
- Break long paragraphs into shorter paragraphs.
- Use lists where appropriate.
- Emphasize details by using white space, boldface, and color for future reference and recall.

According to Maria Veloso, the author of *Web Copy That Sells*, the average visitor to a website stays approximately eight seconds—and that includes click and load time.[9] So if what you're asking people to do isn't easy for them to figure out, they're gone.

Time and time again, I myself have put off automating a particular process or task because either the software instructions made the program look daunting or other users commented that the program was "unfriendly." Yet once I pushed myself past that hurdle of presentation and actually tried the software, I found it simple and fast. The presentation—not the product itself—proved to be the put-off. But nobody said that making something simple would be easy. David Ogilvy is said to have rewritten his famous headline 104 times.

Change in and of itself is hard. Influencing people to change their mind or actions is like building software so intuitive that users no longer need a help menu.

*Simple ideas sell. But making the complex simple—that's hard.*

# 4

# The Law of Tact
# vs. Insensitivity

You cannot antagonize and influence at the same time.
—**John Knox**

How often misused words generate misleading thoughts.
—**Herbert Spencer**

In the heat of verbal battle, you frequently hear someone say, "We're just quibbling over semantics," as if the words didn't matter. Words embody thoughts, shape opinions, and direct actions. They can change the behavior of a few or move a nation. They can sink a stock or launch a war. They can mend a marriage or end a partnership.

Some word choices turn people off because they are tasteless, tactless, or pompous.

Of course, people attempt to change others' thinking routinely by modifying their word choices to sound more appealing. Consider these examples:

- *fund-raising* (noble) or *crowdfunding* (needy)
- *deficit spending* or *generational theft* or *fiscal conservatism*
- *insurance policies with high deductibles* or *sub-standard insurance*
- *layoffs* or *terminations* or *rightsizing*
- *committee* (primarily decision making and authority?) or *task force* (primarily work with no authority?)
- *problem* or *concern* or *challenge* or *issue*
- *oil drilling* or *energy exploration*
- *taxing* or *revenue building*
- *abortion* or *pro-life* or *pro-choice*
- *notebook* or *workbook*
- *rigid decision-maker* or *firm decision-maker*
- *modest home* or *mansion* or *cottage* or *starter home*
- *used car* or *pre-owned car*
- *secondhand store* or *resale shop*
- *outgoing manager* or *flamboyant manager*

Your choice of words can turn the positive into a negative in a nanosecond.

## Avoid Manipulating by Mouthing Jargon You Don't Understand

David Parsley, senior vice president of Brinker International, talks about the frequently misused term *strategic partner*. "What most mean by that is that they want to sell me everything they manufacture with little or no understanding of our menus, our restaurants, or what our guests want." Very few suppliers really become true strategic partners the way their clients understand that term.

To illustrate his point, he cites strategic partner Cargill. At the time the senior vice president at Cargill called on Parsley, they were doing only about $1 million worth of business together—not much for the size and scope of the company Parsley was working for at the time. Ten years after that call, Cargill had developed $100 million worth of business with that company because they delivered on a variety of levels by being what David Parsley terms a *real* strategic partner.

"Why is that? First, they delivered value on the products," Parsley recalls. "They did all kinds of value-added products for us. . . . They were competitive—they earned every dollar they got. They also did commodity-based products for us. . . . Third, they had a risk-management organization to help us control costs. . . . Fourth, they had a global presence. So when we were expanding around the world, they could become a supplier in those countries. But also in other cases, they became an advisor and could help us identify other suppliers we should talk to in these countries. And the fifth thing: They had a presence on the hill in Washington, DC, and could advise us on emerging issues—everything from animal welfare to governmental regulations. They became a real strategic partner."

The term *strategic partner* holds meaning for him. He insists that suppliers know what it means, and mean what they say when they use the term.

## Neutralize the Hot Words

If you ever prepare food in a pressure cooker, then you know that the operating instructions tell you to remove the pan from the heat for about twenty minutes to let the cooker cool down and the head of steam decrease before removing the lid. Take off the lid too soon, and the steam buildup may result in an explosion that sends your food all over the kitchen.

The same thing happens when you try to open closed minds without giving people the opportunity to let off a head of steam built up from offensive words. Never mind your intentions. It's not about what you mean with the words you speak. Their explosion is about what they hear with the words you choose.

Whether the words are tactless, careless, insensitive, or simply misunderstood, if you want to accomplish your objective, aim to neutralize any negative words or phrases that you anticipate will close the other person's mind.

Here are common "hot" words and phrases to avoid when possible:

| Hot Word/Phrase | Replace With |
| --- | --- |
| *audit* | review |
| *prepare financial analysis* | see if this makes economic sense |
| *change* | modify |
| *have a legal liability* | to ensure we are in compliance |

| | |
|---|---|
| *your complaint* | your concern, question, issue |
| *our contract* | our agreement |
| *your payment* | your investment |

## Pay Attention to Emotional Hooks

Forget actor Alec Baldwin as poster child for this principle. Reporters' cameras have caught him insulting people routinely, some of whom he may occasionally need in his corner to make a favorable comment on a movie.

Consider not only emotional control, but also intelligent choice.

For years, marketing researchers have split-tested persuasive words for their marketing campaigns. That is, they send almost the same offer to two control groups, changing only a word or two to see which offer works best. Gregory Ciotti has published a well-researched blog article, reminding readers of the previous studies leading to his list of "Five Most Persuasive Words":[1]

**You:** Of course, we understand the power of personalization and the use of a person's name to get their attention. That's one of the key advantages of customer relationship management tools—the ability to send a mass-mailing to a million people and greet each person by their first name.

But the magic is the same in talking to one individual: To increase your influence with them, call them by name. Use the "you" approach as you write and speak. Make people feel that you're speaking just to them individually.

**Because:** The power of "because" becomes evident if you have children. Your preteen asks to go camping with Johnny and his parents for the weekend. You say no. The first thing out of the preteen's mouth? "Why?" People respond better to almost anything with a reason—even if the reason doesn't make sense. That is, some reasons provide no additional explanation but they still persuade. For example: "I need you to get home before dark because I don't want you to be out by yourself after dark." Or: "Have that report to me by Friday, because I want it before the weekend."

**Free, Instantly, New:** These come-ons need no explanation as motivators. Who doesn't want something fresh and exciting, now, without cost?

Other "big-draw" words that continue to test well: *money, sales, power, benefits, results, easy, proven, guarantee, safety, healthy, bargain, breakthrough, compare, convenience, reliable, common sense, stable, predictability, insight, performance-driven, specialist.*

If words didn't matter, you would open a menu at your favorite restaurant and read items like "tuna and mashed potatoes, served in wine sauce" instead of "sesame-seared, sushi-grade tuna served with parmesan mashed potatoes, tamari wine sauce, wasabi, and pickled ginger." You would attend conferences that promised experiences like this: "Learn from a fabulous lineup of industry experts." Instead, you attend events described like this: "Mix, mingle, and learn from an unparalleled lineup of industry masters, award-winning practitioners, bestselling authors, celebrity keynoters, and world-renowned behavioral scientists."

Whether persuading employees to cut costs, asking a client to extend a project deadline, or inviting family for the holidays, consider your words carefully.

# Phrase to Avoid Unintentional Biases That Create Negative Reactions

Reputation is on the line every time political pollsters conduct a survey. Constructing unbiased polling questions can be tricky, and they know it. You'll notice that when results are announced in the media, three other facts are also typically reported along with the results: (1) who did the polling, (2) who responded to the poll (that is, a random sampling or a particular group), and (3) how many responded.

**Open- Versus Closed- and Forced-Choice Questions:** If the polling organization intends to maintain a reputable standing over time, it has to take key measures to rid the poll of bias by phrasing the statements or questions in a neutral way. For example, open-ended questions will generate different responses than forced-choice questions. Whether the forced-choice response appears in the a, b, c, or d slot matters (so an unbiased poll rotates responses in varying spots).

**Biased Phrasing:** How you phrase a question can dictate the response you get. The same can be said of assessments—personality assessments, management assessments, skill-based assessments, career-aptitude assessments, and IQ assessments. Several questions inside the assessment aim to "balance" for bias.

Once again, different phrasing leads to different interpretations and often very different responses.

**Real Numbers Versus Percentages:** With numbers, phrasing matters as well. Real numbers are stronger than percentages. "Four out of five managers" sounds like more than "80 percent of our managers." "Your risk of a shutdown with this machine is under 5 percent" sounds like much better odds against failure than "fewer than five out of one hundred clients ever have to call us with a shutdown on this machine." The brain processes percentages as an abstraction. People or items seem more real and thus have a stronger impact than an abstract percentage.[2]

**Specific Versus Rounded Numbers:** Specific numbers sound more authoritative than rounded numbers. But rounded numbers are easier to remember. So when you intend to build a strong, persuasive case and also want your listeners to remember what you said, combine both phrasing approaches. For example, if you're displaying a presentation or writing a document, use the specific number (26.3 percent). As you're summarizing, say, "About one in four of our customers prefer . . ."

Savvy speechwriters, copywriters, counselors, journalists, and consultants don't just drift into dialogue, draft copy, and deliver. Having studied the principles of persuasion, they know the outcome they want and how they plan to get there.

You can do no less. If you want to bypass the pitfalls of turning people off to your message, filter phrasing that shows bias, carelessness, or insensitivity.

## Draft Phrasing for a High-Risk, Emotional Situation

When you face a particularly high-risk conversation and fear that emotions will run high, take your planning process one step further: Actually draft what you plan to say so that thoughtless words will not make the situation worse.

This lifelong practice of mine has served me well in many situations with customers and family: Calling an important client that is not paying a long-, long-overdue invoice. Terminating an employee. A parent-teacher conference. A merger discussion. Strategic-partner discussions.

Even though it takes time to literally plan and write out your phrasing, it serves several good purposes:

- You can remove the emotional words and stay with factual words.
- You have time to double-check for accuracy.
- You have time to let your draft "cool off." This cool-off period allows time for review to make sure you are including appropriate details and deleting irrelevant information.
- You have a record of what you said—and didn't say.
- You don't get sidetracked by unimportant issues "in the heat of the moment."

Authors Ronald Shapiro and Jeff Barker published *Perfecting Your Pitch*, which has as its core premise what I'm suggesting here. The three steps outlined in their book include (1) draft, (2) play devil's advocate, and (3) deliver. The bulk of their book suggests conversation guidelines, which I highly recommend, for various tough situations—everything from talking to a poorly performing employee to suggesting that an elderly parent hand over the car keys.[3]

The time involved in this drafting effort is not wasted. Rather, planning your phrasing can represent the difference between success and failure in making your point without making an enemy, in influencing without insulting, and in building a case without blowing up a deal.

## Spin Up Rather Than Spiral Down

Quite often when you're persuading someone to change in some way or building your case for some key recommendation, your listeners push back with *"Yes, but . . ."* The resulting discussion spirals downward until it comes to a complete stall. For example:

- "If we raise membership dues by another $500, we'll have at least 30 to 40 percent of our members drop out of the organization. We're already charging more than most of our sister organizations."
- *"Yes, but* our costs have gone up year after year. And we haven't raised dues to stay up with our costs."
- "Members don't care what the costs are. They just have an expectation of what the membership is worth, and they aren't going to pay more for it."
- *"Yes, but* we're offering more benefits year after year."
- "We have to stay in line with other sister organizations."
- *"Yes, but* those organizations don't offer the subscription services we offer, or access to the conferences without additional charge, or . . ."

You see the impasse here. The "yes, but" comeback stalls progress. Instead, try a different tack by spinning up with a "yes, and" approach:

- "If we raise membership dues by another $500, we'll have at least 30 to 40 percent of our members drop out of the organization. We're already charging more than most of our sister organizations."

- "*Yes, and* that really sets us apart. What could we do to make people feel their membership is worth that extra $500?"

- "I don't know. We already offer everything our sister organizations do—and probably more. People just can't afford to pay more."

- "*Yes, and* they will be scrutinizing the benefits carefully to see if maybe they should drop one organization or the other. I suggest that we try to incorporate a couple of other low-cost-to-us benefits—but things they consider high value. This might encourage them to drop their other memberships and put all their eggs in one basket, so to speak—ours."

- "What if they don't, and we lose 30 percent of our members the first year?"

- "*Yes, and* that's a possibility we should consider if we go through with the increase in dues. Timing will be important. We should add the new subscription benefit first and announce the no-tuition conferences before announcing the increase. Then, if membership drops, I suggest that for the first year, we build on the draw of exclusivity of the organization."

You cannot move people to change their mind as long as your conversation moves in a tit-for-tat pattern. Pushing, insulting their intelligence, invalidating their opinions, and creating an argumentative tone leads nowhere. If not toward agreement, the "yes, and" approach has to move the discussion at least sideways.

## Recategorize to Make the Old New

Sometimes ideas, products, services, or approaches fall out of favor. They become not only unpopular but downright repulsive. People feel insulted, put off, or offended when such a word or term moves from the good column to the "tasteless" or "insensitive" column.

For example, many high schools, colleges, and professional sports teams took the names of various Native American tribes. And today, some people consider the use of these team names as offensive.

Years ago, many people considered "muscle" cars (cars built in the 1950s through the 1970s, designed for high-performance driving) as prize possessions. Today many people perceive such cars as detrimental to the environment. They are offended that other drivers own them.

Do you remember when "refined," as it relates to food, used to be a good thing? Now "organic" gets the rave reviews.

To influence people to take another look at an old idea—or at least one that's become commonplace—either rename it, recategorize it, or rebrand it.

We do it with foods: Potato chips and corn chips are now "veggie chips." Milk shakes are now "healthy smoothies." Pasta dishes are now "pasta salads." (One restaurant chain where I often eat now has a six-ounce sirloin and broccoli on their "lite" menu at 250 calories and the "salads" on their regular menu, sporting 650-plus calories.) Prunes are now "dried plums." Sodas are now healthy "sports drinks." Popsicles and ice creams are now branded yogurts, squeezables, and fruit bars.

We rebrand leisure activities: Exercise is now Zumba, spin, metabolic conditioning, Pilates. Staying at home rather than going on a trip is now glamorized as a "stay-cation."

We recategorize learning and self-development: "Reference manuals" have become "learning aids." "Practice exercises" have become "games." "On-the-job" training has become "just-in-time" training.

We recycle management philosophies: "Management by walking around" of the 1980s is now "hands-on" management. "Management by objectives" has evolved into "Six Sigma processes." The executive's "open-door policy" has now morphed into "online engagement with customers and employees."

Recategorizing works wonders to refresh a stale and often unpopular or even offensive idea or product.

## Call the Authorities

Sometimes your own words prove not to be persuasive enough to move the needle. No matter what positive words you choose, how you phrase the idea, or whether you rebrand the old concept, others have still not changed their mind or taken the desired action.

Consider using other authority figures to deliver your message and up the amps. The term *expert* no longer carries the cachet it once did because so many people claim the term for themselves. So you may refer to real authorities in any number of ways that carry weight with your audience: "specialists," "award-winning practitioners," "intellectual property attorneys," "satisfied clients of ours," "celebrity golfers," "patent holders," "members of the President's Top 1 Percent Club."

Look for ways to weave comments from qualified authorities into a recommendation, speech, website, meeting, or conversation. You can interview them and share their comments, quote their writing, share their blog post, or distribute their white paper. If they join you in holding a point of view that has fallen into disfavor and controversy, you have added to your persuasiveness. Such social proof underscores that you're not the only person who believes in the product, service, change, or idea.

*Words will work—if you make them. And positive, powerful, tactful words work best of all.*

# 5

---

# The Law of Potential vs. Achievement

I only have the power of persuasion.                    —Donald Trump

More than a decade ago, I received a call from someone who'd left his job with a Fortune 500 company to become an entrepreneur. He had received coaching from some of the best in the industry about how to make it as a motivational speaker. In fact, for the past couple of years I'd heard him referred to as a "rising star."

He had just inked a book deal, and was phoning to ask me to be the writer. I let him know that, while I was flattered, I was busy writing my own book and didn't take ghostwriting jobs. I offered to recommend someone else, and asked what the book's topic was.

"I don't have a topic yet," he replied.

"What do you speak on?"

"Just . . . motivational. Have a positive attitude. That sort of thing. I'm going to have my agent call you. She has some ideas for what I could write about."

Later, both his agent and the acquiring editor phoned me to

discuss ghostwriting the book. Through other channels, I discovered that he had received a $750,000 advance—a hefty advance even in the days before publishers put the skids on such advances for business titles that never earned back the up-front payment.

This untested author earned a hefty advance for an unwritten book on an undetermined topic at a time many excellent established authors earned less than a tenth of that fee for their work.

People are willing to risk more and pay more for potential than achievement. The ability to sell a dream or couch your recommendations in terms of potential payoff expands your influence.

## Position the Allure of Potential

If you intend to persuade people to change their mind or do something that involves personal credibility or competence, you will generally find it easier to sell them on your potential than on actual achievement. The reason: the allure of the unknown payoff.

Before examining your own experience, let's delve into the studies behind this preference. Zakary Tormala and Jayson Jia, from Stanford University, and Michael Norton, from Harvard Business School, conducted eight studies to understand this counterintuitive preference.[1]

Consumer behavior research reveals that people are willing to pay more and buy sooner when they feel certain, rather than doubtful, about products and services.[2] On the face of it, evidence of performance should reduce uncertainty about someone's talents and increase confidence about the future. Potential, by contrast, should increase uncertainty and risk, thereby lowering confidence in someone's future success. Someone with only potential might succeed—but might also fail.

For those of us who might want to influence others, the researchers raise this provocative question: Is it possible that highlighting a person's achievements can be *less* effective or compelling than highlighting a person's mere potential?

In their first two studies, Tormala, Jia, and Norton focused on sports and leadership. Seventy-five undergraduate students were asked to imagine that they were managing a team in the NBA with the intention of offering a contract. Two "candidates" were given ideal stats, with this difference: One candidate had already achieved these stats. For the other candidate, the stats were presented as "performance *projections*." To counter the argument that other facts about the candidates' background might make a difference, the rest of the candidate profiles rotated as they were presented to each of the seventy-five study respondents.

In the second experiment, the researchers replicated the study, but in a different context, with eighty-four participants recruited through an online database: hiring hypothetical job candidates. One candidate had two years of relevant experience and scored high on a test of leadership achievement. The other candidate had no leadership experience, but scored high on a test of leadership potential. Other facts in their profile rotated between the candidates.

In both studies, participants preferred the candidate with "potential" over the one who had actually achieved results.

The researchers continued to test their hypothesis through six additional studies in different contexts: Evaluators judged paintings and the artists who created them. They placed Facebook ads and evaluated comedians as to their perceived believability and credibility.

They asked participants to review one-page letters of recommendation for applicants to PhD programs in business and then evaluate the applicants.

In all cases, the evaluators preferred potential over achievement.

My own interviews with executives confirm this phenomenon as well. While some pointed out that it is an even better return on investment to hire "potential" rather than achievement (rookies demand a lower salary), they also agreed that hiring "potential" often has an allure of the unknown.

Tried-and-true, long-term performers have been tested. The organization knows what these candidates can do—and has probably seen the *limits* of what they can do. An untested, new performer is like a blank canvas. Although the new hire may fail, there's also the chance that he or she may succeed beyond all expectations. If the organization can pay this new hire less money than the tested long-termer, the risky hire of the "potential" may be the best business decision, after all.

You may have experienced the same thing in your own dealings or observed the same decisions implemented by others: A new supplier seems to have more potential for meeting your needs than the incumbent. Sports teams pay rookies disproportionately higher salaries than superstars already signed. Hollywood stars with one current hit movie sign the next contract for twice what the four-time Oscar winner has earned per film.

As one California businesswoman remarked, "Silicon Valley pays for an idea. They see value in the next bright, shiny solution. Their mantra is 'fail fast.'"

So, according to these Stanford and Harvard researchers, the reasons for this counterintuitive preference come down to this:

- Potential is more interesting than achievement precisely because the outcome is uncertain. (That's why games, contests, or lotteries generate excitement.)
- Potential entertains us. We're involved as we see how things evolve. (Watching "achievement," on the other hand, is like seeing a movie for the seventh time.)
- Potential engages us because it demands deep reasoning. (As things progress, we mentally scrutinize the pros and cons of our decision—much like watching a chess match on which we have placed bets.)

You may recall this "potential" preference yourself relative to holidays or vacations: Have you ever heard someone say, "I had more fun the last six months *planning* our vacation than actually making the trip"? Anticipating the *potential* trip proved to be more interesting, engaging, and entertaining than the actual travel.

So what does the preference for potential over achievement mean when it comes to presenting your own projects and ideas, particularly where personal credibility becomes part of the equation?

## Consider Crowdfunding for Capital

Whether you need only $7,000 for a hobby "project" that could develop into a serious part-time business, or $250,000 to manufacture and market your first widget, consider the success behind the fund-raising projects on websites such as Kickstarter, EarlyShares, Indiegogo, Fundable, SeedInvest, and Kapipal.

The model for these start-ups is focused on potential. While investors show interest for many reasons (shared values, the opportunity to invest, and "spreading the word" about products and services they believe in), the mental challenge to anyone visiting these sites to evaluate this or that project as a worthwhile investment proves thrilling.

Can you present your own projects, ideas, recommendations, changes, and their potential outcomes in an equally tantalizing way?

## Let Customers Have It Both Ways

Some consultants, contractors, and entrepreneurs have identified how to win by letting their clients consider both angles—potential and achievement—as they make purchase decisions. They offer their services to clients on either a commission-only/pay-for-performance basis *or* as a firm up-front fee. As a result, they attract clients in both categories: Those who prefer potential are engaged by the upside promise of outstanding performance. They are willing to pay more for outstanding results; they owe little or nothing if stated goals aren't met. Those who prefer certainty pay a set fee for a definite task. Goals may or may not be reached.

## Look for the Upside in Your Christmas Stocking

Last Christmas my young grandson solemnly watched as Santa handed out the gifts under the tree to the other siblings. Two, three, four, five—the gifts for his siblings and cousins kept piling up while he sat alone with his one box. Seeing that he looked more and more intent as the moments ticked by, I finally said, "Jake, something wrong?"

"No . . . ," he said, "I'm just thinking that if the others are getting all those presents, there must be something pretty valuable in my box here."

Likewise, contractors can set their clients, and themselves, up for a similar proposition of potential value: the commission-only or firm-fee arrangement discussed earlier. They win either way because they have confidence in their past achievement and future potential. Even though under the first option they will not receive up-front payment, they don't see such arrangements as high risk. The upside may be higher-than-normal compensation for the service because they require no guarantee of payment and because all payment comes at the end rather than at the start of the project.

Several of my colleagues collect their fees as stock options in the client companies they consult, as a percentage of savings they achieve for the clients they consult on a given project, as a percentage of revenue generated from an idea they give to a client, or as a higher-than-normal sales commission rather than a base sales salary.

The choice falls to whoever has the greater confidence—and who can be the most persuasive.

## Write Your Résumé With Potential in Mind

Yes, résumés should summarize what you've accomplished—specifically, accurately, persuasively. But that does not mean that they cannot also highlight what the past jobs, projects, and achievements have positioned you to handle in the future. Always include the significance of those achievements and make them as quantifiable as possible.

## Position Your Career Advancement by Highlighting Potential

When making a career move inside their organization, people tend to talk about being a steady performer. They talk about tasks, tactics, and experience. But what most often tickles a new boss's ear is potential—vision for what can be done differently. Have you studied the area you'd like to move into? What's working well now? Where's the pain? What's the impact of those problems? What's the cost of the problem? What have they tried that didn't work? What ideas do people have that have not been fully implemented? What new ideas do you have? What have you seen work in similar departments or organizations?

Steady Eddy is . . . well, steady. But to move up in the organization, tantalize with your potential to solve a problem, restore morale, or simplify systems. That's your inroad.

*You're limited only by your creativity in putting the principle of potential to work. Consider what you can package as your own untapped potential. And if you're trying to influence others to make a change, encourage them to focus on the potential for success. While potential does represent risk, it also generates excitement about a fresh start.*

# 6

## The Law of Distinction vs. Dilution

Persuasion is better than force.                    **—Proverb**

Leadership is influence.                              **—John Maxwell**

**Scenario 1:** You're a committee member at your professional association, putting together an incentive bonus to encourage members to
renew their $399 annual membership four months early. Here are
things at your disposal that you could offer:

**A:** 30 percent discount on the $399 membership fee

**B:** 30 percent discount on the $399 membership fee, plus a $10
discount on registration at the next association meeting

**C:** 30 percent discount on the $399 membership fee, plus a $10
discount on registration at the next association meeting,
plus a $5 discount coupon toward any product offered on
the association's e-store

Which offer will generate the most renewals in this situation? Please make your choice, and continue to follow along through the remaining scenarios.

**Scenario 2:** You're putting together a press kit for a new book by a previously published business author. Which items would you include?

**A:**
- book overview
- names of three previous bestsellers by this author and their sales records
- literary award on the author's first book fifteen years ago
- favorable testimonials by three CEOs of small corporations

**B:**
- book overview
- names of three previous bestsellers by this author and their sales records
- literary award on the author's first book fifteen years ago

**C:**
- book overview
- names of three previous bestsellers by this author and their sales records

**Scenario 3:** You're preparing a formal presentation to the executive management team to persuade them to relocate the business. Actually, there are many good reasons to move the business, but you're limited to a fifteen-minute time slot. How many of the following reasons should you present to the management team to get a positive decision?

**A:**
- less expensive per square foot
- more prestigious address
- equivalent drive time for most employees (so the move would not generate a negative reaction)
- More compatible tenant businesses that may draw more attention to yours

**B:**
- less expensive per square foot
- more prestigious address
- equivalent drive time for most employees (so the move would not generate a negative reaction)

**C:**
- less expensive per square foot
- more prestigious address

**Scenario 4:** Your company wants to discourage employees from parking in emergency lanes around the company facilities. You and your committee are charged with designing a company policy that would penalize violation of the "no parking" zones. Your committee has discussed the following combination of penalties. As part of your policy, which penalty would likely be perceived as the most severe?

**A:**
- $500 fine
- three hours of community service
- loss of company gym privileges for a week

**B:**
- $500 fine

**C:**
- $500 fine
- three hours of community service

**Scenario 5:** You've just opened a new resort. You're offering guests who book rooms for the first month the following two incentive packages—Package A and Package B—on two different websites to test which brings in the most business:

**Package A:**
- 20 percent discount on a seven-night stay
- all meals in the dining room included
- free rental on all water-sports equipment
- free shuttle transportation around the island

**Package B:**
- 20 percent discount on a seven-night stay
- all meals in the dining room included
- free rental on all water-sports equipment

Which package will most likely generate the best reaction to your resort?

According to the research, here are the best answers in the above scenarios (we'll analyze why a little later):

**Scenario 1:** A: 30 percent discount on the $399 membership renewal

**Scenario 2:** C: Book overview, names of three previous bestsellers and their sales records

**Scenario 3:** C: The lease costs less per square foot. The address is more prestigious.

**Scenario 4:** B: $500 fine

**Scenario 5:** B: 20 percent discount on a seven-night stay, all meals in the dining room included, free rental on all watersports equipment

## Understand the Presenter's Paradox Principle

Are you surprised by the answers above? If so, that's possibly because these scenarios set you up as the "presenter" or communicator of the message—not the listener. We perceive situations, value, and penalties quite differently—depending on whether we're *communicating* them or *hearing* them.

The natural tendency for communicators is to think that more is better. (That's why it's so easy for parents, managers, or leaders to lapse into lecture mode!) Human nature leans toward excess. If thin is healthy, then thinner is healthier. If pricing on the regular soft drink makes sense, then the super-size drink seems like a steal. If jogging three miles a day keeps you in shape, then training for a marathon should make you superfit. If investing $20,000 in this start-up is a good deal, then why not sink half your life savings into it?

People transfer that same thinking to the workplace when they prepare a résumé, write a sales proposal, describe product benefits, launch a marketing campaign, or tout their favorite political candidate. They go to excess. In a résumé, they try to list ALL their past accomplishments or credentials. In the product description, they list ALL the features and benefits. In the sales proposals, they list ALL the reasons to deal with their organization. Their reasoning? "Well, it's an extra; it can't hurt."

But it does.

More is *not* better, according to the Presenter's Paradox studies.[1] When presenters offer extra "benefits," the offer does not necessarily have an additive effect. Often the "extra" cheapens the perceived value of the overall benefit and even subtracts real value—as measured by what a customer is willing to pay for a product or service. At best, the low-value "extra" may leave a negative impression of the high-value benefit.

> The natural tendency for communicators is to think more is better. . . . Human nature leans toward excess.

What prompted these seven studies by the Presenter's Paradox researchers was a situation many travelers encounter today—an airline delay. One of the authors of this study was seated on an airplane when, after a two-hour delay for mechanical trouble, the airline announced that passengers would have to deplane and switch to another aircraft. In an effort to accommodate disgruntled passengers, the airline offered a gift package: a thirty-five-dollar discount coupon toward future travel, a meal voucher, a premium beverage or mileage bonus, and a phone card for what amounted to about five minutes of talk time. The author thought the package "cheap" in that the phone card didn't even allow enough talk time to make alternative travel arrangements.

The question raised by this offer: Was the airline spending money in an attempt to communicate an apology but in reality creating a worse impression overall? That question began a series of research studies in which the authors tested several similar situations— scholarship packages offered by major universities, bonus giveaways with product purchases, hotel amenities, and penalties for littering.

Here's what they discovered: When making an offer, communicators intuitively think more is better. They consider each item as a single add-on component, increasing the value of the whole offer or message or apology (as the case may be).

But listeners don't look at the situation in the same way. Instead, they "average" all the pieces of information they hear and walk away with a single impression. The same premise held true whether the messages were positive or negative, or whether the "bundled" offers involved similar or dissimilar items, or whether all were monetary or non-monetary items.

Not only did "more" add less; it actually harmed the rest.

## Don't Make Averaging the Contagious Choice

This principle of "averaging" may even play havoc with your customer satisfaction ratings. In a recent interview, here's how one auto insurance customer reflected on her experience after a recent car accident on the way to work:

"The insurance agent did a great job. Excellent customer service. Then they asked us to do a six-question electronic survey at the end of the transaction. Everything the agent did was great: She answered all my questions. Gave me information on a local body shop to get my car repaired. I would have given all excellent 5 ratings, had question 6 on the survey not reminded me about timeliness.

"The agent promised the interaction would take us about twenty minutes, and it actually took almost forty minutes to handle their paperwork. Adding that last question reminded me about timeliness. Did they really want to know how *fast* the agent handled the transaction—or how *well*? So in the end, they left me with the feeling of, 'Well, maybe not so good, after all.'"

In my interviews with other executives, this "excess" effect surfaced in multiple ways: One executive at a manufacturing organization remarked, "A few details can derail a board discussion. When presenters think they are being comprehensive, they are really taking us off target by providing information we don't need."

He went on to add, "On the procurement side, when we rank suppliers in a bidding process, we pay attention to the most important criteria. When we go to market, we have a formal system and put it all in a formal list to create a level playing field. But some bidders insist on adding things. That just irritates. It detracts. Most often, it lowers their ranking."

Here's how this "dilution" or "averaging" reasoning works in another specific situation. Let's say you're preparing your résumé to apply for a position with a consulting firm. Based on your research and an initial conversation with the potential employer, you know the hiring executives value results and experience in the field. They also demand appropriate academic credentials. You also heard them comment on their new push to generate more leads through published articles, so you decide it can't hurt to mention that you previously published two white papers a few years ago on employee retention.

So you list several credentials in a draft copy of your résumé:

- Led two client organizations through bankruptcy proceedings back to healthy profits and annual growth rates above 20 percent within three years
- Served as project manager at Deloitte Consulting for fifteen years, handling projects for $50 million to $500 million clients in turnaround situations, in which deadlines, budgeting, and staffing were critical to success of the organization as a whole
- Earned an MBA in business and finance, Wharton School of Business
- Published two white papers on employee retention

But the Presenter's Paradox studies suggest that the potential employer will not "add" that fourth credential to the stronger credentials. Had you stopped with the first three credentials, the evaluator would have rated you like this:

**A+** Consultant at two client organizations, leading through bankruptcy proceedings back to healthy profits and annual growth rates above 20 percent within three years

**A+** Project manager at Deloitte Consulting for fifteen years, handling projects for clients in turnaround situations, in which deadlines, budgeting, and staffing were critical to success of the organization as a whole

**A+** MBA in business and finance, Wharton School of Business

With the first three credentials, the hiring executive is thinking they've discovered a top-notch candidate. But after adding the fourth credential, the applicant has weakened the impact of her résumé. The evaluator "averages" the credentials this way:

**A+** Consultant at two client organizations, leading through bankruptcy proceedings back to healthy profits and annual growth rates above 20 percent within three years

**A+** Project manager at Deloitte Consulting for fifteen years, handling projects for clients in turnaround situations, where deadlines, budgeting, and staffing were critical to success of the organization as a whole

**A+** MBA in business and finance, Wharton School of Business

**C-** Author of two white papers on employee retention *(Minor achievement, several applicants have published white papers, and the topic is not of interest to us.)*

As a candidate, she "averages out" to a "B+" rather than an "A+" contender for the job.

This principle meets resistance among many job applicants. But, being frequent victims of hype in résumés, hiring executives understand the subtractive principle. One of the communication training programs my firm has created and delivered for IBM is how to write consulting biographies. As part of that consulting project, I reviewed myriad biographies. It always amazed me that an executive could summarize a stellar thirty-year career in three or four bullet points— while a two-year consultant needed seventeen bullets!

Know when a plus becomes a minus.

## Consider Perceptions Above Reality

Once again, this latest series of seven studies done by the Presenter's Paradox researchers corroborate the same conclusion that many previous studies have shown: Influence is not about what you *say*, but what listeners *hear*.

Let's get specific with the analysis. We're talking about impressions.

In the opening Scenario 1, a 30 percent discount on a $399 membership fee creates the overall impression of a deep discount. To add a measly $10 off registration to another meeting or the $5 off a product cheapens the deep 30 percent membership discount ($100) offer.

A further point the research shows about bundling offers: While the person offering the bundle is adding up the value of each piece in the bundle and discounting an amount from that total, buyers often expect to pay *even less* than the most expensive item in the bundle![2]

In Scenario 2, with the press kit for the bestselling author, including three previous bestsellers with a proven track record of sales on these bestsellers makes a *huge* positive impact. To toss in testimonials from three unknown CEOs and an award won long ago on a prior book simply dilutes the focus. The "averaging" rule sets in to diffuse the overall impressive credentials.

In Scenario 3, about relocating the business, tossing in the fact that commuting time for employees will not be a factor is a moot point. While it might quell concern about negative reaction from employees, it certainly would not push executives toward a positive decision. And moving to a location where you have tenants with a similar clientele would rank less important than the other two. Again, the executive audience would "average" those four reasons to give them a B motivation for the move. Had the executive team examined only two reasons for the move (lower cost and prestigious address), the "averaging" effect might have earned an A priority.

In Scenario 4, adding the three hours of community service and losing privileges to the company gym for a week simply weaken the impact of the $500 fine for the "no parking" violation. Again, the listener is "averaging" the components, not adding them. The impact of the $500 fine hits harder when heard alone. The penalty gets diluted when the listener "mixes" the fine with a "no big deal" reaction to losing gym privileges or participating in community service.

In Scenario 5, the vacationer who reads resort Package A is likely to have a negative impression of the resort—rather than the intended positive impression. A likely reaction of those reading this package:

"What? Only shuttle service? At this price for an exclusive resort, they should provide a free private car service or reimburse for a taxi!" For those reading Package B *without* the mention of transportation, vacationers see the total package as high value.

Recall your own role as *receiver* of communication. You've probably experienced this "more is not better" thinking all too often. Consider that experience as you apply this counterintuitive principle.

## Reduce the Length of Presentations and Speeches

Do you remember being in the audience during an awards ceremony when a one-minute thank-you speech would have been great, but a five-minute speech bored everyone to death? That's almost always the reaction during the Oscar or Emmy awards presentations, and it provides the next day's TV talk-show host with filler discussion. At eighteen minutes, the international TED Talks have become famous not only for their content—but for their brevity.

## Cut the Clutter in Slide Design and Number

As a professional speaker, I'm frequently invited to speak at industry conferences where a marketing team has prepared a "slide template" for all guest speakers to use in preparing their presentations. Some are well designed. Most are not. They contain logos, a visual theme for the event, and often a slogan for the event. All this clutter leaves little room on the slide for anything else.

Slides should be a visual representation to support your key point. If they have words on them, those words should be few and of high value. This is no place for ten bullets or three sentences or a chart of statistics.

Limit the number of slides as well. The presenter with five great visuals engages an audience; the presenter with sixty-five slides puts an audience to sleep.

## Scrutinize Your Signs

"I wish people would just pay attention to the signs!" It's a common complaint of customer-service agents. But the fact is that many signs contain so much information that customers cannot easily find the information they want. It's simply too time-consuming and cumbersome to wade through the clutter.

Exhibitor booths at trade shows serve as one of the best (worst?) examples of product and service dilution by displaying everything the organization has or does rather than communicating a distinctive, clear message for a single audience and occasion. Every year as I walk trade-show floors, I find few exhibits that clearly communicate what their organizations offer.

Consider your favorite casual dining restaurants: It can take ten minutes to go through the menu. Have you ever tried to wade through your insurance policy to see if you're covered for some specific surgery? Have you ever passed up a billboard that had too much on it to read before you whizzed by?

The test is not to see how much text fits into a space—but how much of a concept you can stick into the brain.

## Make Customers Do Website Interviews

Ask likely customers to go to your website for the first time and then watch them navigate. See where they get lost. See where they give up and leave. Yes, I know tech people have tools to see where visitors enter your website and at which point they leave. But you actually want to see those people—eyeball to eyeball. You need to see their furrowed brow, grimace, hesitation, puzzlement, and weariness in reading, rereading, and trying to digest what you've written.

Following their exploration of the information there, interview them. Ask them the key questions you'd like them to remember. If they don't pass the interview test, your website has failed.

## Avoid the Over-Helpfulness Syndrome

Although not a common disease among customer-service reps, this OH syndrome (over-helpfulness) does attack nice people from time to time. Case in point: My computer technical-support specialist was in the office to help with installing a new customer relationship management (CRM) system and import all our contact records. While he was waiting to run some reports, I asked him a couple of unrelated technical questions. "I'm also Microsoft certified. If you want me to correct that while I'm here, I can do that. I'm also a phone specialist. Here's an idea for you. Would you like for me to set up your phone so it will do . . ."

He left eight hours later, having "helped" with many things but leaving me confused about how all the changes, installs, and plug-ins actually benefitted me.

The same scene often unfolds in on-the-job training, classroom training, and written help manuals. Instructors and documents often provide so much information that they dilute the usefulness of their help.

So, no matter whether you're discussing poor performance with an employee, making a sales presentation, talking to your boss about a raise, writing copy for your website, or designing an incentive award package for top salespeople, consider this counterintuitive principle: Listeners *average* rather than add components in a message and walk away with an overall impression—valuable or not valuable, high value or low value, strong or weak offer.

*The next time you're faced with this more-is-better temptation, squelch the urge to splurge. Communicate more with less. Subtract to add.*

# 7

## The Law of Specificity vs. Generalization

Communication will never make a bad project good, but bad communication can fail to convey the benefits of a good project.

**—Tom Hund, CFO, BNSF Railway**

You don't have to be a "person of influence" to be influential. In fact, the most influential people in my life are probably not even aware of the things they've taught me. **—Scott Adams**

Quick pop quiz here: No research allowed.

What brand comb or hairbrush do you use? What company makes the mug that you drink coffee or tea from every day? What brand sofa do you sit on to read your favorite books or watch TV?

I'm guessing you couldn't answer these three questions—unless you're in the business of selling or manufacturing hair products, coffee mugs, or furniture.

But three more questions here that you're sure to answer in a snap: What brand of cell phone do you use? What kind of car do you drive? What soft drink or sports drink do you choose most frequently?

When you think of soft drinks, do you think of either Pepsi, Coke, Dr Pepper, or Sprite? When you think of cell phones, do you think of the iPhone or the Android? When you think of cars, do you think of Ferrari, Porsche, Lexus, BMW, Mercedes?

So what's the difference between the first and the second set of questions? Specificity. Uniqueness. Despite the fact that the items in the first group are familiar products used every day, no single brand has become a household name. Items in the second group have made themselves stand apart from their competitors. They have touted specific features, benefits, or advantages that have set up a contrast with other products or companies on the market.

The same can be said of individuals. Those who set themselves apart in some specific way develop a brand, gain mindshare, and become influential when they spread ideas.

"Often employees who have aspirations to move up have not decided what their strengths are or what their real experience is," observed Han Kieftenbeld. "They'll come into my office and say, 'I'm looking for something else. I've worked three years in sales. I've spent two years in IT. I've done a tour in R&D. If something opens up, I'm interested. Keep me in mind.' I'll do nothing with that. Basically, they've had a generic career. They need to assess and be specific."

Whether people, products, or services, the age of generalization has passed. Specificity stands center front.

Randomness terrifies people. In a world where someone can walk into a shopping mall and open fire on hundreds of innocent people, where jobs disappear overnight, where cancer appears suddenly on an X-ray, people grasp for control, order, and stability.

They expect the same from communication coming to them—

that it should make sense for them personally. When generic messages bombard them, they shut down or push back.

All of the following comments have one thing in common: They are generic comments that can be—and often are—used in many different situations. People use these generic comments as if they are on automatic pilot. None move listeners to change their mind or feel more positively about a situation. In fact, such statements anger people, cause them to dig in their heels, and stall action:

*"It's our policy. That's the best I can do."* In the midst of negotiations, this ultimatum typically brings the situation to a halt—unless the other person really has no other options. And rarely is that the case.

*"We will get back to you when we have a resolution to the problem."* When leaders toss this promise to a crowd during a crisis, they react with, "We want to know *now* what you're doing to find the resolution."

*"We regret the layoff situation as much as you do."* When employees being terminated hear such a statement, skepticism replaces trust.

*"I'm sorry that you feel this wasn't explained adequately."* When managers deliver this comment to customers, they argue that it wasn't their "feeling" but a *fact* that the issue wasn't explained.

Take apologies, for example. We've all heard apologies from athletes, movie stars, politicians, or CEOs caught in some wrongdoing. Generic apologies sound forced, insincere, and lacking in personal

When random, unshaped messages bombard us daily, they make us want to tune out. accountability. Those apologies stay in the news for days—or decades. By contrast, effective apologies move people to forgive because they sound sincere, are relevant to the situation and audience, and make amends. In a word, they are *specific*.

Like apologies, any information that influences and persuades people has to be specific.

## Provide Context for the Not So Obvious

You climb into your car, turn on the ignition, and look at the gas gauge. The black needle points to the halfway mark. Is the gas tank half-full or half-empty?

Your answer, of course, depends on context. Let me elaborate:

If you thought the car was empty and you were twenty minutes late leaving for work, and were expecting to have to stop for gas, you will be pleasantly surprised. You'll notice the gauge and breathe easier, thinking, "Ah, it's half-full. I'll fill the tank later tonight after work."

But what if you had filled the gas tank completely two evenings ago as you came home from work? The next morning you intended to crawl into the car and leave for a long weekend out of the city. You didn't want to waste a moment stopping for gas but intended to beat the traffic to the expressway. You turn on the ignition and discover the gas gauge at the halfway mark. In this case you probably see the tank as half-empty.

To understand how context and description interplay to work on your brain, consider those questionnaires financial advisors send clients as they set up their investment profiles. They may ask you outright about your comfort level with risk (conservative? moderate? aggressive?). But they'll never take you at your word. Instead, they send you a survey of scenarios that frame those labels:

**Which Portfolio Would Be More Acceptable to You?**

   **A.** A return rate of 8 percent over three years with fluctuations of no more than 12 percent in any one year?

   **B.** A return rate of 25 percent over five years with fluctuations of up to 40 percent in two of those five years?

Those financial firms describe and frame situations to capture the real truth about your comfort with risk and volatility. Their questionnaires make risk and reward relevant to your day-to-day peace of mind and stress level. They force you to think specifically: "Can I sleep if my monthly financial statement looks like this?"

Context and description become essential as you position ideas for others to consider, approve, decide on, and act on. Pity the poor staffer who hears this general directive from the boss: "We intend to keep our customers happy. Use your own judgment if you have to make a quick decision and I'm not around."

Considering the context, an online customer-service agent might interpret the use-your-judgment directive to mean she should refund the shipping charges if the customer insists. But a sales rep may interpret the use-your-judgment statement to mean she should grant the customer a full refund for merchandise he himself damaged in use. A sales rep with a national account may interpret the directive to mean she should give the customer a 40 percent discount on his annual bulk order, thus destroying the total profit margin.

Context matters.

## Curate Your Content

Although a current buzz phrase, "curating your content" applies equally to your grandmother.

The Internet provides access to free information from everywhere. But that's not always helpful. In fact, because the information is overwhelming, it can be unhelpful. Even with the search engines, the massive amount of random information can be too much. A search on Google for *persuasion* will take you to 9,560,000 sites. A search for *love* will lead you to 4,120,000,000 places. Granted, we know how to filter search strings on the Internet. But how about when you're on the receiving end of communication?

In the days before the Internet, telecommuting to work, and the globalization of the workforce, you could expect to influence others through your personal presence alone—face-to-face. But those opportunities decrease every month. To move people today, you have to communicate online for a specific audience. If you don't, they unfollow, unfriend, or unsubscribe.

Curating or sorting is the point behind your online communication. You are the filter for your followers. You influence by what you filter to them: your conversations, presentations, writing, shared posts, original posts, white papers, videos, audios, podcasts.

How far does your influence reach? That depends on several things:

- Platforms (distribution channels such as social media, TEDx, HuffingtonPost.com, Forbes.com, the *Harvard Business Review*)
- Exposure (hitting people over and over until they decide to act)
- Frequency (of blogs, tweets, posts, books, articles, emails, other media appearances on TV and in print)

Just keep in mind that to move people, they have to hear from you. Find your fans, discover where their interests intersect yours, and then filter your information flow to them.

## Match the Other Person's Reality

Despite all the talk about globalization of markets and business, that's not the experience of the typical individual. Do you wake up every morning thinking, "I wonder if the crop situation in Kenya is improving?" "Have taxes gone up again in Uruguay?" "What's the GDP in Cambodia this quarter?"

Yet many executive speeches miss the mark because they aim for the general workforce and hit no one. As Jane Binger, senior researcher and frequent advisor to C-suite officers in the health-care field, commented: "Change messages particularly are written at the 30,000-feet level. They don't even puncture the average person's reality—their day-to-day world. People are managing 200 hits a day to their email box. Executives have to get their attention first."

Indeed. People react to their own information flow and items in that flow that pique their interest. Operational people (IT analysts, accountants, human-resource specialists, purchasing agents, quality-assurance managers) react to operational news and glitches.

Salespeople and customer-service agents react to client news, industry trends, and service problems so that they can advocate for the customer. Executives keep their eyes on the financials, trends, and competitors because they need to answer to shareholders.

This experience approximates watching the same TV news broadcast day after day or reading only one newspaper.

To influence such a wide audience involves merging their streams of information into one river. You, as curator of part of their content, can open and close the floodgates at will to help merge the flow of new information into their streams.

Consider whom you are trying to influence—specifically. Match their emotional mood. Open the gate at the appropriate time. Make it real and relevant for best results.

## Toss a Big Tent Over Your Discussion

When you expect disagreement with an opinion, start with a broad shared universal goal or truth that anyone can accept:

*"We all want to see this campaign succeed."*

*"No child should have to go to bed hungry."*

*"Companies need to make money to stay in business."*

*"Our suppliers should be able to count on us to deal with them honestly and fairly."*

Such an opening statement disarms people who intended to push back. It instead sets the tone for consensus on what's to follow—as if the details on "how" are minor details to be worked out. Then you set about to influence them on the details to follow.

## Give Relevant Reasons in the Right Order

Often, in working with those in staff positions (accountants, attorneys, analysts, marketers) in client organizations to help them prepare presentations or proposals, I'll hear them say, "But I don't need to give the reason for my recommendation; the reason is obvious. It'll save us $x$ dollars" (or increase productivity, or whatever reason they think is obvious).

But when I have the opportunity to talk personally to their executive audience, that intended audience retorts, "It's not obvious to me! They may be looking at the dollars, but I'm looking at the overall value" (or whatever criteria that executive might have in mind).

In fact, people are more inclined to do what you want when you say the word *because*, even if the reason doesn't make sense or simply states the obvious. This idea is borne out by research by one of the foremost authors on persuasion, Robert Cialdini.[1] His classic work, *Influence: The Psychology of Persuasion*, identifies six elements of persuasion: reciprocation, commitment and consistency, social proof, liking, authority, and scarcity. Providing a "reason" communicates authority.

When teaching technical writing, I caution learners not to reason in circles with statements like this: "Further analysis was delayed, pending more testing, because further testing will provide more insight into probable causes." Does testing ever give less insight? Such "reasons" are non-reasons, but people respond better when they hear such "reasons" even if they are nonsensical. People fail to think through the logic of what they hear; they simply react to "authority."

What is obvious to the speaker or writer is seldom obvious to the other person.

If you're speaking to someone you expect will agree with you or one you think will be neutral, present your strongest reasons first. If you're speaking to a group or an individual who will be opposed to what you have to say, start with your weakest reason and build to the strongest point. This arrangement leaves them with the feeling that each argument is growing stronger and is more difficult to overcome. Finally, at the end, they cannot refute your most convincing reason.

Make an exception to the above structure, however, if you have doubts that the skeptical listener will stay with you until the end. You don't want the other person to abruptly stop listening (or reading) before you've had the opportunity to get to your strongest point.

In most business settings, that is the case: Decision makers want the bottom-line message quickly. In those situations, state your point, then prove it, with your most persuasive points first.

Structuring your message appropriately is paramount. Present negatives *only* after you've commented on the positives or the benefits of your idea, product, or service. Above all, never go back and forth between pros and cons. That kind of wishy-washy structure serves only to leave your audience confused.

If you happen to be invited to participate in a marathon of meetings, don't get stuck in the murky middle. Instead, choose to go either last or first, the places of strongest attention and best recall.

(Thorndike's Laws of Primacy and Recency are discussed in my earlier book *Communicate with Confidence, Revised and Expanded Edition*.)

## Tell *How*, Not Just What or Why

"Save for retirement now." "Cut costs so you have money to invest when the market is strong." "Study hard so you can get a scholarship." "Lose some weight. If you don't, you're going to have some major health challenges just like your dad."

People often hear outcomes like these and really want to heed the advice.

The problem turns out not to be *what* they need to do, or even *why* they need to do it. The reason they see no progress when both you and they have the same outcome in mind is that they simply don't know *how* to accomplish the goal.

Instead of continuing to state the *outcome* you want, give them the how—suggest some specific steps to help accomplish the goal or change. Shift your attention to a workable plan. Not a thirty-seven-step plan. Not even a twelve-step plan. Step back and focus on a few priority activities that you can persuade them to do that will lead to the final goal or decision.

### For Example, Tell Them HOW to Save for Retirement Specifically

- Increase your 401(k) contribution to 4 percent.
- Move into a smaller home.
- Sell one of your cars.

**For Example, Tell Them HOW to Lose Weight Specifically**

- Stop eating dinner so late in the evening—no later than four hours before bedtime.
- Exercise at least thirty minutes a day, five days a week.
- Eat five servings of veggies or fruit every day (no sugar added and none fried).

# Keep Their Actions Consistent

People like to believe that they're consistent in what they think, value, say, or promise. It affirms their own trustworthiness and credibility. Once people say they believe in something—a person, a cause, an organization, or an idea—research shows they will do their best to respond consistently.

For example, you've probably watched pundits in the media defend the actions of a public official they've helped put in office. They will continue to defend, support, and explain away gross incompetence or egregious moral lapses—all because of this need to feel they are consistent. Their reasoning goes like this:

- "I thought he was a good guy back then, so he's probably still a good guy."
- "I recommended her for the job six years ago. I cannot be wrong now."
- "This charity made sense to me when I read their website. We have the same values. Nothing important has changed. The mission is still the same. Therefore, I'm going to send my money to them."

This consistency principle is at work when people ask you to click a post, visit a website to vote in support of an issue, or forward an email to someone in support of their cause. Later, they ask you to write a letter or provide names of your friends for others to contact about the cause. Finally, they ask you to send a donation or volunteer your time to serve on a task force.

Put this principle to work by pointing out a specific past action and asking the other person to repeat it. If you're soliciting funds: "You were kind enough to contribute $500 last year to our efforts. Can we count on you this year for that amount—or maybe even more?" If you're working in sales: "The last time you ordered, you bought a year's supply; I'm assuming you want to do the same this shipment?" If you're talking to your college student: "You've always made good grades because you know that's your ticket to a high-paying job after graduation. So I know you're going to buckle down and study for these last two exams. Giving up because the professor is difficult just wouldn't be like you."

Once people support or agree with a cause or goal, they find it difficult to be inconsistent.

## Make It Personal

When applied to communication, relevance by definition means making your appeal relevant to the person. Research shows that the simple act of adding a personalized Post-it note request asking people to complete a time-consuming survey prompted significantly more and higher-quality responses than those without a personal sticky note.[2] The authors of the study concluded that when a request feels specific and personal, reciprocity again plays a role in subconsciously compelling people to respond—even when they don't know the person making the request. This reciprocity appeal activates more frequently in some people than in others. (I'm raising my hand here.)

If you ask for a favor, make it something easy to do by giving all the specifics: Give a phone number or address to a colleague, directions to the closest sushi bar, an explanation about "how the association really runs." Once others invest time with you in this small way, they're more likely to do so again. Later, when you want to build on the relationship to discuss an issue—for example, to ask them to change something you disagree with, to present a product or service—they feel more inclined to listen.

Connection and an investment of time increase your chances to persuade.

## Create the Future

"I could never do that." "That's not in the cards for me." "I can't afford that." When you hear these comments from people, you know they lack vision. They consider a certain outcome either impossible or irrelevant.

To influence them, your challenge is to make that future seem attainable and applicable to them in particular. If you're trying to move them toward a positive change, create vicarious modeling experiences so that they see specifically how things *can* turn out well. They need to interact with and model people who have made the change. These interactions may happen in various ways: through learner exchanges in a classroom, between workers on the job, by watching skilled performers on YouTube or TV, by hearing testimonials recorded on a website, or reading firsthand experiences in a book.

On the other hand, you may need to help someone catch a glimpse of the painful future if they don't make a change: a retirement with insufficient funds saved, their failed company because of poor customer service, their decreasing paycheck because of wasted sales time, their series of dead-end jobs for lack of an education, or their loss of a close relationship due to an addiction.

Create the experience in full detail with all the specifics for them to visualize and consider. Let them interact with people living that future life. Find stories of firsthand experience for them to hear.

Once they have reached the emotional state you intend for them, walk them back to the present day with ". . . but it doesn't have to be that way; you can still make the change. There's time."

## Anchor Your Point

Why do items often cost $19.95 instead of a round $20? Because precision packs a punch.

That's the issue researchers Chris Janiszewski and Dan Uy, marketing professors at the University of Florida, investigated as they ran a series of tests to explore why retailers didn't just sell items for twenty dollars and save us all from having to make change. They discovered that people appear to have a subconscious mental calculator that prefers precision to randomness.

In one test, the researchers checked five years of real estate sales in Alachua County, Florida, comparing list prices and actual sales prices of homes. They found sellers who listed their homes with precise pricing more consistently got closer to their initial asking price than those who started with a rounded number ($378,600 versus $380,000).[3]

Precision, whether in pricing or otherwise, keeps people grounded to a particular point. Retailers use this technique routinely when they tag merchandise: "Compare at $97.99. Today only $69.79." Retailers anchor to that higher price point of $97.99 to add perceived value. The specificity of the 79 cents communicates that buyers are getting a special deal—not the usual 99 cents deal.

Using this anchoring principle to start a discussion dramatically increases your chances to stay focused there at the end of the discussion: For example:

> **You:** "Do you think we'll have more than 200 employees enroll in our tuition-reimbursement program?"
>
> **They:** "I haven't looked at the potential numbers yet. We could go higher than 200."

Chances are strong that the discussion that follows will center around the number 200—if for no other reason than that was your opening number. If your first sentence had mentioned 2,000, the discussion would have centered around a number higher or lower than 2,000.

Another example of anchors:

> **You:** "Were you expecting something different than the 3.6 percent profit our bid proposes?"

**They:** "I can't say I was expecting less than that. But 3.6 percent will be tough this year."

That percentage will be the anchor that forms the centerpiece of the discussions. If you had started the discussion at 5.2 percent, you likely would have had the same discussion, with the higher percentage anchoring the discussion.

Random, wide-open discussions provide no context. Anchoring your discussion with relevant, specific details—whether discussing pricing, recommendations, or management issues—leads to a persuasive conversation.

## Make Pain Less Intense

No matter what you're trying to influence someone to do, negatives typically enter the picture. Solutions are seldom pain free. Change usually involves a period of chaos until people struggle through it to success. Even the world's most powerful software requires a learning curve.

Influencing people to take action or to change their mind often includes minimizing as much as possible the potential pain of a negative outcome.

If you're selling things, you can reduce the pain of risk several ways:

- Make a "try before you buy" offer.
- Give a generous, "no questions asked" returns policy.
- Post written guarantees (people like to "see it in writing").

- Post your privacy policies.
- Tell people they can trust you! (Research says simply telling them to trust you inspires trust.)

You can also minimize the pain of parting buyers from their money in these additional ways:

- Bundle things so they can pay once for multiple items.
- Don't nickel-and-dime buyers by adding on small fees for this or that after the primary sale. Otherwise, the pain keeps coming over and over again.
- Provide different payment options and terms. Not all buyers can handle the big lump payment.
- Detach the pain of paying with the act of buying by using the "bill me later" option, the "simply click here" option, or the "get four months free and just write 'cancel' on the invoice" option.
- Accept credit cards or direct withdrawals from their bank accounts (people don't feel the pain of paying so much if they are not parting with the actual cash).
- Drop the dollar sign in front of the number. (Current research has shown less resistance to pricing without the actual $ showing.)[4] Notice menus in upscale restaurants—many no longer display the dollar sign.
- Add decoy items to increase perceived value. (Notice one or two extremely high-priced items in a catalog or on a restaurant menu. These are not meant to sell, but to add perceived value to what buyers actually select at a lower price.)[5]
- Add decoy items to increase perceived quality. (Offer better-quality items for almost the same price as lower-quality items.

These high-quality items decrease pain because buyers perceive the higher value.)

Whether talking about an idea, a project, a product, or a service, ask yourself this key question: How can I make this decision less painful and the change more positive specifically for this one customer?

Forget selling to the "everyman" and "everywoman." Ask questions. Dig deep. Get specific.

- What's the other person's perception of pain? (Paperwork? High cost? Excessive regulations? Taxes? Micromanagement? Risk? Fear of failure? Embarrassment?)
- What's the other person's perception of quality or a positive outcome? (No stress? Speed? Fun? Praise? Longer lasting? Time off? A raise? Durability? Dependability? Ease? Easy to learn? A loving relationship? A better education?)

Answering these specific questions with relevant information makes for a persuasive conversation.

## Make Your Delivery Mode Specific

Have you considered the physical setting for persuasive conversations? One executive friend of mine drives five hours out to a farm, where he sits all alone on what he calls his "thinking stump" to contemplate important decisions in the organization. Should you choose such a getaway place to converse with someone on an important topic? Or would he or she consider that an inconvenience and an embarrassment to be called away from the office, causing others to ask questions about their absence?

Some people think, work, and play best with music playing in the background. Others find background music distracting.

Influence that drives change proves more successful when it syncs with personal preferences: the listener's *specific* work habits, body rhythms, body language, communication styles and modes. Research on all these angles has measured the direct impact on a purchase decision.

In fact, of Internet browsers searching for lodging at a resort, those listening to jazz more often chose cozy hotel rooms (80 percent of the time). But those listening to music with a heavy drumbeat chose outdoor accommodations far more often (camping, youth hostels, and the like. Only 5 percent of this music group chose hotels.) And only 12.5 percent of the control group (no music) chose hotel accommodations.[6]

Roger Dooley reports these takeaways from various studies on the link between body language and influence cited in his excellent book, *Brainfluence*:

- Music (of all types) affects buyer behavior.
- People have a right-ear preference. Requests made to the right ear are likely to be more successful.
- When buyers see a smile in an ad or from the salesperson, they buy more and are willing to pay more for what they buy.
- Your marketing should include every human sense: sight, sound, taste, smell, touch.[7]

If you're using multiple media and multiple channels to influence others, how well do your webinars, social media posts, and videos meet the above criteria? If you're asking people to carry a heavier workload, how can they find a suitable atmosphere to make them most productive?

After you craft a compelling message, take care that you select the specific way to deliver it: Who should deliver it? Should it be delivered orally or in writing, by email or letter? When is the best time to deliver the message, have the conversation, or make the announcement?

The delivery specifics can either destroy or enhance your message.

*Generic information no longer influences people. In fact, they will dodge it. To be influential, curate your content into a meaningful flow. Specificity builds contrast and draws attention.*

# 8

# The Law of Emotion vs. Logic

Compelling reason will never convince blinding emotion.
—**Richard Bach**

Storytelling is the most powerful way to put ideas into the world today.
—**Robert McAfee Brown**

Consider how your emotions change quickly with the circumstances: Do you feel the same on a gray, cloudy day as on a bright sunshiny day? Do you feel different on a holiday than on a Monday-morning commute to work?

Think about the decision to buy your house or rent your apartment: When you first walked into the place, how did you begin to evaluate? Did you love the ample kitchen cabinets for storage? Was it the cozy fireplace, the picture-window view, the nearby hiking trails, or the backyard deck that got your attention?

Research shows overwhelmingly that we base our buying decisions on emotion, and then support them with logic. In a business setting, a logical argument is expected, of course. Just don't expect the logical argument to win people over.

In *The Heart of Change*, John Kotter and Dan Cohen discuss a study they conducted with Deloitte Consulting about the nature of change. The study involved more than 400 interviewees from 130 companies in the United States, Australia, Europe, and South Africa.[1]

Their interpretation of the data? Even in large corporations that focus on very logical approaches to strategy, culture, and analysis of data, change happens because the leaders find a way to help people see problems or solutions in ways that influence their emotions, not just their reasoning.

If someone uses a reasoned argument to rationalize why they have decided to do $x$ instead of $y$, don't let the explanation mislead you. The logical explanation offered for deciding to do $x$ often has nothing to do with the underlying emotional decision. The logical explanation merely justifies or supports the emotional decision that has already been made.

Does this mean that to be persuasive, you should use an emotional appeal in *all* circumstances? Of course not. Just as with any other powerful pull, an emotional appeal can be misused to manipulate others. Listeners can be led to decide against their better judgment— especially when they are depressed or when they need your approval. When that's the case, the manipulator may feel guilty and ashamed. In some situations, the very fabric of influence becomes flawed.

Even with that said, your aim to persuade will rarely be easy, because people have a tendency to believe what they want to believe.

Researchers published a study in the *New England Journal of Medicine* that suggested sham knee surgery yielded the same benefits as the real surgical procedure. This knee surgery treats tears in the meniscus, the cartilage that acts as shock absorber between the upper and lower portions of the knee joints. The Finnish researchers studied two sets of patients—those who received the surgery and those who were led to believe they'd had the surgery.

The control group that did not receive the actual surgery had tiny incisions made in their knee, and the doctors used instruments to press against their knees to mimic the real surgery. Although there was a slight decrease in pain early on after the procedure for the surgery group, there were no significant differences in improvement between the two groups of 146 total patients after one year.[2] In other words, some believed their knee felt better—whether or not they'd had the surgery. Others believed their knee did not feel better—even though they had had the surgery.

Once again, this study emphasizes the power of emotion to control the mind. All the situations mentioned here simply underscore the power of emotion. Used wisely and with integrity, your emotional appeals can have tremendous power to sway people.

## Speak to the Heart

Leaders soon discover that people cannot hear logical reasons for change in an organization until they work through the emotional issues surrounding that change. Researcher Shaul Fox, writing on the power of emotional appeals in promoting organizational change, identifies five "domains" that touch listeners' emotions:

- The core message
- Phrasing of the messages

- Characteristics of the leaders
- Interaction of the leaders with those going through the change
- The setting[3]

Take, for example, layoffs. Fox goes on to report the difference in the emotional impact in a semiconductor manufacturing plant based on the metaphors used when employees were told about the plant closing. At first, employers heard leaders use this metaphor: "turning out the lights." Employees perceived the decision to be insensitive and disrespectful of them. The bitterness deepened when the media started referring to the plant closing process as "handing out pink slips."

But later in the process, the predominant metaphor was changed to "the grieving process" for those who remained and had to see their friends leave. Some at the site began to see the closing more positively, as a natural process they had to cope with as in other areas of life. They began to heal and move forward. On the other hand, other employees reacted differently to the "grieving" metaphor. They focused on their loss and could not look forward.

Tom Hund talked about leading a change situation at BNSF Railway: "We do the majority of the economic analysis for the company in our Finance department. When we first started doing that, many of the users (Marketing, Operations, HR, Labor Relations, and so forth) had always done their own analysis. But we as a company concluded that there was no standard way of doing this, and that we should put all of this analysis in Finance.

"A number of people considered this *taking away* their decision-making capabilities. So first, we had to sit down with them and say, 'What we want to do is develop a standard way for *you* to have better information. As a matter of fact, we need *you to tell us* which variables are most important to you. You need to tell *us* what your sensitivities are, so we can devise a plan to *give you information* to make your decision. We want to help *you* have a standard way to know that if you trade, say, a rate increase for some type of other concession, *you'll know* the value of what you're trading. But we're definitely not *taking away* your decision-making capability.

"So now they have standards that they're using company-wide. They wouldn't even think of going to the negotiating table without running this economic analysis process. It's second nature."

Cost-cutting situations also commonly call for emotional appeals to change behavior. One executive summarized the leadership team's message to employees this way: "'We're not doing as well as we'd planned. And we don't want to lay anyone off. So to keep from doing that, we need you to be cost conscious. We want you to spend money as if it were your own.' It was an honest, straightforward, clear message. We talked to them as if they were family members. Their reaction was wonderful. People came up with hundreds of great ideas. We got the message across with a letter from the CEO, through our regular management structure, and in our briefing meetings. We told them that we were opening up an idea database for them to contribute suggestions. They started contributing immediately, and we started executing on a number of those suggestions. . . . We treated them like family, and they reacted like family."

Metaphors, analogies, straightforward phrasing, examples—all of these are part of speaking to the heart as a leader.

Politicians understand the power of an emotional appeal to move a nation. Consider political slogans from the past:

- *Had enough?*—the 1946 slogan for congressional elections for the out-of-power Republican Party
- *Hey, hey, LBJ, how many kids did you kill today?*—anti–Vietnam War and anti–Lyndon B. Johnson slogan from the 1960s
- *It's the economy, stupid*—1992 presidential campaign of Bill Clinton

It's not only their slogans but their everyday sound bites that tug at the emotional strings—either positively to position their point of view or negatively to castigate opposing perspectives.

Charities, particularly, depend on an emotional appeal—particularly stories—to move donors to action. In fact, researchers Deborah Small, George Loewenstein, and Paul Slovic have done studies that suggest appealing to donors with logic and statistics actually reduces their charitable giving. Their study found that donations were higher if people were asked to support Rokia, a starving seven-year-old girl in the African nation of Mali than if they were asked for money for three million children facing starvation in Mali.

Another twist on the study: Respondents gave less in the Rokia appeal when it included statistical information about the overall starvation problem in the country than when the appeal omitted that statistical data.[4]

Clearly, philanthropic groups want to encourage donors to support nonprofits that use their money most effectively. They understand that giving based only on emotion is ineffective and will not always lead to wise decision making. But they definitely understand that appeals based only on logic do not persuade. Their goal has become to touch the heart of informed donors.

Do you recognize this general outline that many nonprofits use in their appeals?

- What's possible here? (The appeal creates a vision of what the money or support in whatever form can do in the future: Build more orphanages. Expand the hospital's services. Send more missionaries. Help more refugees. Provide more jobs or a better education.)
- Why you? (Why are you the ideal donor to help out? The appeal points out shared values, interests, goals.)
- Why now? (Why is the need so urgent? New laws on the horizon? Dire predictions? Trends surfacing? Personal stories of those in urgent need?)

St. Jude Children's Research Hospital tells the story of one child with leukemia who needs your help. Habitat for Humanity tells the story of one team from the Citadel going into the community using their skills to rebuild one home for the Gonzales family. 6Stones Mission Network tells about providing food, clothes, school supplies, and an apartment for a single mother and her five children for six months until she became self-supporting. They all focus on specific stories that create a vision for how the donor's money and time will be spent.

Whether you're talking about change, political campaigns, or charity, when you want to move people to action, speak directly to the heart.

## Lower the Bar on Fear

Calm the emotional reaction of fear: *It's too hard. I can't finish the project on time. I can't master this job. I can't change that habit. I can't save enough money to afford your product or service.*

Your challenge: Make change easy by reducing the distance to the goal.

Airlines do it. Credit card companies do it. Restaurants do it. In fact, it's difficult to find any place of business today that hasn't learned this principle of persuasion.

Airlines persuade passengers to sign up for their frequent-flyer programs by depositing bonus points into their accounts when they enroll, putting them well on their way to their first mileage award. Credit-card companies enroll new cardholders by offering 25,000 bonus points on their airline partner's frequent-flyer account—again, putting them "almost there" for an award. Department stores give shoppers a "punch card" for buying socks: "Buy a dozen and get the next pair free." And then they punch two holes on the card with the first purchase to get the shopper well on his way. Restaurants use the same punch-card offer. Newspapers and magazines use the same strategy: "Subscribe for a year—and we won't even start the meter for another month."

"Raising the bar" may work with a few overachievers, but most of us like to be successful from the get-go. Change seems difficult enough already. So your job is to reduce the size of the change: How can you make change seem less monumental, even small?

## Apologize Sincerely and Promptly

Beware the power of negative emotion to dwarf your influence and stall change. Handle potentially negative situations with care.

Catherine Hernandez-Blades knows the power of a sincere emotional appeal to turn a negative situation around. As chief marketing and communications officer for her organization, she made a media buy months ahead of time for a "cover wrap" with a national magazine.

When that month's issue of the national magazine hit her desk with her CEO's face on the wrap, it was over the face of the magazine's memorial issue for an industry giant who'd passed away that month—the CEO of one of their top ten clients!

Understandably, people at her organization were upset—the CEO, the board. Panic broke out.

"Give me thirty minutes," Hernandez-Blades said. She dashed to her office and drafted a letter to the client's board of directors: "We had no idea when we placed the ad months ago that we would lose a pioneer of our industry. . . ." The language was very sincere, very deferential, very respectful. They sent the letter to all members of the client's board of directors.

The client's board responded favorably to the letter. Had the language and tone not properly addressed the emotion of the situation, no logical explanation would have been sufficient to control the damage.

One of the biggest threats to people or organizations today is the power of negative emotion going viral. An irate customer or a few, with a little creativity, can put you out of business almost overnight. Put that negative emotion online and the damage spreads exponentially.

Find a way to say yes to negative emotion. If you burrow deep enough into the negative emotion, comment, or complaint, you will typically find something you can agree with to turn the situation around. Instead of "We can't do that; the cost is prohibitive," you might turn the situation into a positive with, "Yes, I can see that will be a problem. Let's think about options for you in this situation."

Emotions between leaders and their own employees run deep—and last long. That negative emotion may linger much longer than people can recall the specific words that generated it. If you don't believe it, ask those who interview job applicants for a living. They can tell you how often applicants vividly recount bad experiences with past bosses—and still get emotional in the retelling.

Emotions—between employees and their boss, between service agents and customers, between salespeople and operations people, between project team members and their leaders—can negatively affect any attempt to reason with them or influence them to cooperate.

By all means, guard against generating this flood of negative emotion that will block forward movement in leading people to change their behavior or their mind.

## Consider Storytelling a Basic Skill for Success

We share our stories with our friends, family, and strangers on Facebook, LinkedIn, and Twitter. We talk about vacations, holiday get-togethers, office projects, and travel mishaps. We don't dump statistics on our social media sites; our stories carry emotion. They drive a point deeper and deeper into our psyche.

We tell ourselves stories about why we do what we do . . . about why we act the way we act . . . about what we said and why we said it . . . about how something should be done or not done. The stories that go on in our head prove positively that stories are a natural mode of communication.

So it should be natural that we tell others our stories as a means to influence them.

When tragedy strikes, the media doesn't just report how many people died, the impact on the Richter scale or the economy, and the inches of snow, rain, or flooding. Instead, reporters find the people stories. They put a face on the tragedy by telling you of the single guy who jumped from the safety of his boat to save a drowning two-year-old whose parents, unable to swim, stood on the swollen river's shore, screaming for help.

But storytelling is not just about sensationalism.

Researchers have discovered that even judges and seasoned attorneys prefer story briefs to logo briefs (those built totally on logical argument). An empirical study on the power of story determined that stories are persuasive to experienced lawyers and judges because they evoke emotional responses that make the legal claims of the parties more credible and elicit empathy in their judicial thinking.[5]

Structure is to storytelling what framing is to a house. Without it, you just have a heap of supplies on a vacant lot.

Think back to your high-school or college English classes. Your professor defined a story this way: "A hero struggles to overcome obstacles to reach an important goal." Keep these tips in mind as you start to build your personal or business stories:

- Show, don't tell. That is, don't tell your audience about the movie. Put them in the movie theater. Re-create the scenes.

- Start with a hero. Anything or anyone can be a hero in the story: your organization, a product, a location, your client, a passerby.
- Don't always try to be the hero or heroine in your own stories.
- Give your hero a goal or challenge to overcome.
- Add struggles. The hero must overcome struggles or obstacles to master the challenge or meet the goal.
- Use dialogue. Let listeners hear the characters talk to one another.
- End with the resolution that motivates your listeners to action.
- Make sure your listeners can identify with the hero.
- Be interactive in the telling.
- Use analogies, metaphors, and props in the telling.
- Be vulnerable. Don't always tell about your successes. Audiences relate more often and learn more from "failure" stories.
- Add humor—self-effacing humor is best.
- Create a callback line. Is there a line from your story that you can refer to later to bring to mind again and again for your listeners—a reference phrase that will continue to drive home your point?

Master this basic skill of storytelling as a first step to move people emotionally.

## Beware the Backstory

As you aim to influence others, consider their backstory as the context for your communication with them. Webster's defines *backstory* as "a story that tells what led up to the main story or plot." Novelists create backstories (or background stories) that are events in the characters' lives leading up to the primary plot. When I write novels, the backstories on my main characters sometimes run up to ten to twenty pages.

Bits and pieces of the backstories may be revealed as the primary plot moves along through dialogue, flashback scenes, straight narrative, a character's memories, or summary. Occasionally, none of the backstory ever finds its way into the primary plot; it serves only to help the writer reveal a character's personality and motivations. On the other hand, the backstory may be so well developed that it's sold as a novel or movie in its own right, a prequel to the primary story.

Your organization and employees had a backstory before they joined forces. Your customers and suppliers had a backstory before they became your customers and suppliers. You and your spouse had a backstory before you married. Each backstory is powerful.

Using other people's backstory as a frame for your message can be a powerful way to unlock hearts quickly and move them to action. Disregarding that context can be disastrous. A frequent misalignment between message and backstory happens when publicly owned companies deliver financial results to Wall Street.

Tom Hund talks from experience about his backstory and the difficulty in aligning it with Wall Street: "We know we have to reinvest in the railroad to keep it strong—locomotives, track, and so forth. We're owned now by Warren Buffett, and he's a great owner to have because he has the long-term perspective.

"But back when we were a public company, there were many times when we would have to go to Wall Street and explain our capital spending. There would be times when we were making investments in the future—five years out. And Wall Street analysts would be looking at the expenditure and ask, 'Why are you spending this money? Why don't you just pay a special dividend to the shareholders with this money? Get it to us now.'

"We'd say, 'But we're not thinking of just this quarter. We're planting seeds for not just this quarter, but for what's going to grow ten, fifteen, twenty quarters out.' We'd end up with a misalignment of time. . . . When I was heading up Investor Relations, I'd explain it this way: 'When you have a publicly held company, you have owners and you have renters. You have to run the place for the owners, not the renters—the guys who move into the stock for a quarter or two.'"

If you're trying to position your entire corporation to customers or suppliers, you may also want to tell your backstory. (For an example of Booher Consultants' backstory and how my intellectual property grew into a communication training firm, go to booher.com/aboutus.)

Some people write their backstory in an autobiography, telling what shaped them from their earliest beginnings. Others create a movie from their business backstory—from start-up to "overnight success." Others put their backstory on YouTube, in their brochure, or in their TV commercial.

In general, businesses have one of three major backstories:

- We saw a need and we filled it.
- Gee whiz, we built this cool widget, and everybody beat down our door to get one. Who knew this thing would catch on?

- We're a no-frills business that has grown from zero to hero due to hard work, customer focus, and smart decisions. If you want it done well at a fair price, come see us.

Add your specific details to these themes, and you have a specific backstory that touches people emotionally and makes them want to root for your success.

As customers, coworkers, or suppliers identify with you, you will have the opportunity to influence them. And stories deliver the same impact in your social and personal life as they do in business—most often, a stronger impact, because friends and family members know you more intimately, care more deeply, and trust you more fully.

## Adopt a "Cause" to Create Connection

"Go green." "Cure cancer in our lifetime." "Feed the refugees." All these causes tug at people's heartstrings. If you tie your message to a cause that people believe in, the emotional connection grows stronger. Every year, my local CPA firm, McIlvain & Associates, creates an event around a race and walkathon in the Dallas–Fort Worth Metroplex to raise money for cancer research. They invite all their suppliers, clients, and employees and their families to contribute and participate personally. As another example of this kind of "cause connection," each spring and fall a Texas utility company pays for the necessary building supplies and allows its employees time away from work to renovate two houses for disadvantaged residents.

## Personalize With a Photo

Adding a photo is not about ego; it's about research. Simply linking a person's photo to dry data increases the connection and changes the results.

Researchers set out to determine if adding a patient's photo to their file would affect how radiologists interpreted the results. For the study, 318 patients referred for CT scans agreed to be photographed prior to their exams. Those photos were then added to their files so that they automatically appeared when a patient's records were opened. After interpreting the results of the exams, fifteen radiologists were given questionnaires that asked about their experience. All fifteen reported feeling more empathy toward the patients after seeing their photos.

But more important, the results showed that these radiologists provided a more comprehensive reading of the CT scans. Incidental findings were reported about unexpected abnormalities found on an image that may have health implications beyond the scope of the original exam.

In order to assess the effect of the photos on the interpretations, eighty-one exams with these incidental findings were shown in a blinded fashion without the photos to the *same* radiologists three months later. Approximately 80 percent of the incidental findings originally reported with the photo-accompanied scans were *not* reported on the second reading. The radiologists involved in the study commented that the photos were a factor in how meticulously they interpreted the images and in their feelings as caregivers.[6]

Marketers also know that baby pictures light up people's brains. Attractive women draw attention in ads. Cute puppies evoke an emotional response. (Need quick proof? Post photos of puppies and babies on Facebook and watch your "likes" skyrocket.) Whatever you can do to create a pleasant personal association increases the persuasiveness of your message.

Influence needs a face.

## Engage Multiple Senses

Strengthen your persuasiveness by involving as many senses as possible to reach the listener's emotions.[7] Of course, different approaches will depend on whether you're communicating face-to-face, on the phone, or online. Here's a starter list of additional ideas for emotional connection through the senses:

- Add tools to your website for visitors to enter their own data. Provide tactile ways for people to connect and play:
  - Calculate how much visitors can afford to pay for a mortgage.
  - Find out how much users need to save each year to be ready to retire well.
  - Assess household income and expenses to see if the family qualifies for student assistance.
  - Give a writing assessment to see if they could benefit from a refresher course to snag that next big promotion.

- Turn testimonials into real anecdotes by video or audio record-ing people telling how they benefitted from your product or service.
- Encourage people to become part of a "tribe" or "community" (call it "elite," "platinum," "VIP," "mentees," or whatever fits). Feeling like they belong to a special group will increase their emotional connection.
- Ask listeners directly, "What are you hoping to achieve? What's your goal? How would $x$ make your job easier, safer, faster?" Their answers engage them emotionally.
- Give people opportunity to touch and feel your offer. The tac-tile sensation makes a strong impression on the brain. How can people do a "test drive" of your intangible service?
- Let people hear firsthand experiences from your employees about how they've coped well with a change, handled a prob-lem, benefitted from a conference or training course. Consider the YouTube craze, with an estimated 100 hours of video uploaded to YouTube every minute. More than one billion unique users visit each month. Viewers don't care so much about the imperfect video quality. What they demand is authen-ticity. Share these firsthand experiences in meetings or coach-ing sessions, or on your website with prospects and clients.

Engagement controls so much of our reaction to what we see and hear that it's difficult to overemphasize its impact on our emotions—either positive or negative.

## Put Emotion Into Your Presentations

To take advantage of the emotional triggers that influence an audience, recognize that you do indeed need to *move* an audience. Often presenters in my workshops argue this point. They'll say, "But what about when I'm just giving information?"

My response: "Yes, *what* about it?" And they look at me blankly, as if they've made their point, so what else needs to be said.

Refuse to think of any presentation in terms of simply informational. (Okay, I'm sure there may be an exception or two. But those will be rare.) Discover the core emotion behind your information or message. For example, I frequently keynote on the topics of executive presence and leadership communication. The emotions people feel related to those two topics include:

- Eagerness to be on the fast track for promotions
- Excitement about starting a new entrepreneurial venture and knowing they'll need to bring in huge business opportunities at the C-suite level
- Frustration that their career has come to a standstill and they don't know why
- Disappointment that they've lost a huge piece of business

Another emotional driver as I talk about these same topics with executives is often:

- Are you disappointed that some of your people lack what it takes to interact at the C-suite level when they call on your clients?

Talking to HR directors, I might use this emotional approach:

- Are you working far too many hours doing the managers' jobs for them because they don't have the will or the skill for straight talk to their direct reports when it comes to poor performance?

With salespeople, executive presence might be interpreted by this core emotion:

- Do you feel that you lack credibility to call on CEO buyers? Is your paycheck taking a hit because you can't close those big deals?

After you identify the core emotional driver to motivate your audience to listen to what you have to say, then shape your message along those lines. Grab their attention with a question or challenge that focuses on that same emotion. Focus on the *emotional* struggle to solve that challenge or answer that opening question. Finally, continue to stir that emotion to lead them to a solution or action.

*People rarely change their thinking or behavior based solely on logic. And remember that negative emotions can block the inclination and ability to reason altogether. Consider emotional appeals and the power of stories to drive your message deep into the brain.*

# 9

## The Law of Perspective vs. Distortion

All our knowledge has its origins in our perceptions.
—**Leonardo da Vinci**

We are enslaved by anything we do not consciously see. We are freed by conscious perception.
—**Vernon Howard**

Most of the mistakes in thinking are inadequacies of perception rather than mistakes of logic.
—**Edward de Bono**

Have you ever stood in an airport terminal and watched a soldier give his three toddlers one last bear hug before leaving for war? If you've felt yourself choke up, that's empathy. If you've ever listened to someone on TV pleading with a crazed killer holding a family member hostage and felt tension throughout your body, that's empathy.

The ability to feel and understand another person's experiences builds a connection. When you have that sincere connection, others recognize it in your face, voice, and gestures. When in that state, you have opportunity to influence others because they know you have their best interests in mind.

But empathy *doesn't* necessarily mean that you can influence someone for the long term and lead that person to the best outcome—nor that you even know what the best outcome might be.

Perspective is *not* about an emotion—empathy. Perspective is about your thinking capacity to consider other viewpoints. Perspective encompasses your ability to anticipate the behavior and reactions of other people . . . and then communicate with them based on that insight.

In fact, studies done by researchers at Northwestern University, INSEAD, Saint Mary's University, and Dartmouth College suggest that perspective-taking will make you more persuasive than empathy will. In short, their research suggests that it's better to get inside someone's head than inside their heart.[1]

Consider why that might be: Empathetic people may become ruled—and thereby limited—by their emotions. They find it difficult to step outside their biased views. So they often go beyond the "norms" of what's fair in order to give preferential treatment to someone they feel compassion for—even giving up their own rights and goals.

You've seen situations like this yourself: A parent who feels empathy toward an adult child continues to accept disrespectful and harmful treatment from that child rather than persuade the child to behave in a fair and reasonable manner by objective standards. Maybe the adult child refuses to hold a job and continues to borrow money from the parent. Feeling empathy and lending the money, such parents may be limiting their influence on the adult child to get a job.

Another example: An employer gives a poor performer a third, fourth, fifth, and even more chances to change a bad attitude simply because the boss feels empathy for the employee. And in the meantime, the poor-performing employee may destroy the morale and productivity of everyone else in the department. Clearly, the boss does not have the best perspective in this situation—that is, the best perspective to influence the poor performer to change his behavior for the good of the entire department.

> Perspective encompasses your ability to anticipate the behavior and reactions of other people . . . and then communicate with them based on that insight.

People with perspective typically have high self-esteem and don't necessarily look at situations for how things affect them personally. That doesn't mean that they don't have biases. Rather, it means that they *know* they have biases, but don't let those biases limit them. They can step outside those biases and take an objective look at what's fair and reasonable in various situations.

For example, consider coaches (or fans, for that matter) at a sporting event. Let's say Team A has an empathetic coach. If the referees make a few bad calls that result in his team falling behind, the coach may begin to empathize with his players. He may encourage them to "get even" and do whatever it takes as long as they don't incur a penalty. He and the team may get angrier as they fall further behind. At the third bad call by the referees, the players become more demoralized. The coach curses the official and gets thrown out of the game, earning another penalty. They eventually lose the game.

By contrast, the coach for Team B has the ability to take perspective in a game with inexperienced officials making bad calls; he can step outside his emotional upset and assess the situation. While he may also empathize with his players, he takes perspective: *The game is not rigged. This is college sports. These are simply inexperienced officials. What my players need now is something to reduce the frustration of bad officiating. I'll refocus them on executing plays with precision just like we do in practice.* The coach with this perspective has a much stronger chance of influencing toward a better outcome for all concerned.

So what's the key to perspective? Listening. Evaluating. Assessing.

You can't persuade people to change their minds or their actions if you don't know what they're thinking or doing. Is your perception blocked or distorted?

## Listen to What's Not Being Said

A Chinese proverb states, "To listen well is as powerful a means of influence as to talk well, and is as essential to all true conversation."

Let me make a distinction between hearing and listening. To hear is to hear noise, sounds, and even words—but without comprehension, understanding, interpretation, conclusions. Many people can hear words in their own language intended for them—and still not interpret a correct message. Listening with understanding and perception is another matter altogether.

The price of not listening is exorbitant. Ask Apple what happened when they took Google Maps off their iPhone, or ask Netflix what happened when they surprised customers with a 60 percent price increase as they announced that all those customers receiving movies by streaming video as well as DVD rentals would be charged for two accounts at twice the price. Ask the designers of the Affordable Care Act how voters reacted when they were assured they could sign up for insurance on October 1, 2013, on the government website and discovered that they could not even log on and that security had not been tested.

If leaders listen to what frontline agents, customers, and suppliers are *not* saying to them, they may have a new perspective on their business. With that knowledge, they can correct problems, negotiate better deals, expand brand awareness, or influence change.

What questions are people *not* asking you about *your* products and services? Why did your biggest customer not ask about volume discounts for the new year? (Has the competitor been talking to her?) Why did Carlos not protest when he learned his promotion was being turned down? (Does he have an offer from a competitor?)

Why did your brother not ask about the dates for the family reunion? (Is he not planning to attend?) Why are you not getting status reports as usual from your project manager? (Is there a problem?) Why is your boss not giving you feedback? (Is it a timing issue or a performance problem?)

Where there's silence, there's typically a reason.

## Listen to What *Is* Being Said

As I facilitate training programs on communication and negotiation skills, I've noticed considerable differences in how people listen with the intent to persuade:

| Untrained Persuaders | Successful Negotiators |
|---|---|
| Assume they know what the other person is "driving at"; often interrupt before the other person finishes | Listen to the complete thought expressed |
| Become easily distracted, let their mind wander, check email or text messages while others are talking | Practice focused attention |
| Either don't take notes—or take notes only to refute the other person | Take notes on what the other person says |
| Give little or no acknowledgment while being spoken to | Acknowledge what they've heard with expressive body language (eye contact, facial expression, alert body language) |
| Listen for areas of disagreement | Listen for areas of agreement |
| Tune out unrelated information as irrelevant to the discussion | Listen for alignments (name-dropping, referrals, testimonials, recommendations, associates) to make assessments and look for other opportunities |
| State their own needs, goals, concerns, or resistance | Ask probing questions to understand the other person's goals, needs, concerns, resistance |
| Make assumptions and jump to conclusions without clarifying | Ask questions to clarify before drawing conclusions |
| Pay little attention to the other person's body language | Read body language |
| Become uncomfortable with silence; talk far more than they listen | Can be comfortable with silence; listen far more than they talk |
| Show agitation in discussions and react emotionally | Remain calm, controlled in discussions and reactions |

As good listeners, these persuaders gather enormous amounts of information that create opportunities for them to change opinions—of the people they speak with and their own. The more people they listen to, the wider their perspective grows. The wider their perspective grows, the more groups of people they understand. The more groups of people they understand, the more individuals they understand. The more individuals they understand, the greater their chance to expand their influence and change the way they think or what they do.

## Let Others Help You Listen

Consider your contacts as your listening network. Who are the strategic influencers you need to make part of your network—not only because of what you're saying but also because of what they're hearing?

If you work in Dallas or Dubai and your colleagues work in Dover or Dublin—then you'll need to make your interactions more intentional and meaningful: What questions do you need to ask the next time you get on a conference call? What topics do you need to "casually" toss out to hear from the grapevine? What conferences should you attend to catch up with the latest trends?

Becoming a member of a community provides another way to listen vicariously. What are other members discussing? What questions are they asking? What solutions do they need? What are their opinions on the key challenges in the industry?

Do visitors to your website and blog have a place to submit questions? Can they be assured they'll get a prompt answer either by email, in your e-zine, in a chat box, in your user community?

Many organizations have entire departments that monitor online conversations about them and respond to complaints and compliments, identify trends in the industry, and look for needs they can meet with new features and services.

A couple of years ago, my bathroom sink had a tiny hairline crack in it. I emailed Kohler, the manufacturer, to ask what they would do about it. And although it was no longer under warranty, they offered to replace it at no cost. They handled the entire transaction through email promptly, cordially, and efficiently.

So I blogged about their customer-service communication—without letting them know I planned to do so. A few days later, they tweeted a thank-you, referring their followers to my blog. And they repeated the tweet several times.

They were listening to the online chatter for just the right conversation—or compliment, in this case.

## Change the Scenery

With some people, an appeal to either emotion or logic still brings no change. The easiest course is to change their perspective by redirecting them to a new path with different scenery altogether.

Diet programs do this when they sell memberships: "Buy our three-meals-a-day food plan and you don't have to have self-control. Just eat what we sell you." Organizations can reduce use of the company photocopy machine by assigning everyone a required code to control who copies what. Bosses can influence change by mandating that all briefings be delivered in twenty minutes or less with ten or fewer slides.

Is the easiest way to produce the change you want simply to change the environment, situation, or process?

## Listen for the Gaps Between Perception and Reality

As my firm works on various consulting assignments in client organizations, I often see huge gaps between the perception and reality of those involved:

- **Perception of Manager in the Field:** "I have no idea where the company's headed. We never hear from the senior execs."
- **Perception of CEO:** "We communicate, communicate, communicate. We have quarterly updates. The message goes down through regular management channels. It goes out to the field. Our leadership team is very visible in the field."

* * *

- **Perception of the Vice President (warm, friendly, big laugh):** "I'm an easygoing guy. I like people. My boss is great. I love my job. I love working with our foreign customers, and I've been very successful with them."
- **Perception of the President (the VP's Boss):** "His smile looks insincere. I don't know if it's nervousness or embarrassment, but people from other cultures just don't trust him. That's why we lost this latest deal the VP handled."

* * *

- **Perception of the Seller:** "My sales presentation positioned me among an elite group of suppliers. I feel certain that I won over the client with it."
- **Perception of the Buyer:** "That presenter was arrogant—unnecessarily arrogant. In fact, it nixes the entire deal as far as I'm concerned."

Listening and connecting provide the only way to close the gap between perception and reality. Otherwise, you're selling tires to the person without a car.

*Perspective makes persuasion possible.*

# A Final Word

Communication—the human connection—is the key to personal
and career success.                                    —**Paul J. Meyer**

M ost of us will never have to talk someone down from a ledge.
But for those around you, your influence may be a life-or-death
situation. Almost daily, you do have to persuade people to change
their minds or actions.

Your influence—to change how someone thinks, discard a harmful habit, adopt a healthier lifestyle, choose a better way of interacting,
improve job performance, accept and move through a challenging
situation, restore a broken relationship—can literally save someone's career or life.

Powerful, persuasive communication leads to success—personal
success, career success, and organizational success. Communication
cultures are created—not wished into existence. Great communicators model the masters, practice the strategies, and measure the
results.

Spread the message: Words matter.

| Why Communication Fails to Persuade | Why Communication Succeeds in Persuading People |
|---|---|
| **Distrust**<br><br>The speaker or culture creates distrust. | **Trust**<br><br>The culture fosters trust or the speaker takes steps to build trust or transfer trust. |
| **Monologue**<br><br>What the communicator assumes is obvious, is not.<br><br>All communication is one-directional. | **Collaboration**<br><br>Communicators find shared values and goals. They collaborate on changes and outcomes and build bridges to close the gaps in misunderstandings. |
| **Complexity**<br><br>Complex language obscures ideas and priorities. | **Simplicity**<br><br>Clear language sharpens focus and drives action. |
| **Insensitivity**<br><br>Careless, insensitive, "hot" words offend and sidetrack people from the primary message. | **Tact**<br><br>Persuasive people use precise, powerful, yet tactful phrasing. |
| **Achievement**<br><br>People undervalue performance and are less persuaded by the past than expectation and hope for future possibilities. | **Potential**<br><br>People are willing to risk/pay more for potential than past performance. |

| Why Communication Fails to Persuade | Why Communication Succeeds in Persuading People |
| --- | --- |
| **Dilution**<br><br>A long list of advantages, benefits, qualifications, credentials, or benefits looks impressive. So communicators often follow the more-is-better rule, thereby weakening impact. | **Distinction**<br><br>A focus on the core distinctive advantages, benefits, qualifications, or credentials (or penalties) produces high impact. A focus on "the few" actually adds, rather than subtracts, attention. |
| **Generalization**<br><br>Generic information does not make a strong impression and is easily forgotten. | **Specificity**<br><br>To be meaningful and memorable, information has to be specific, relevant, interpreted, and structured to fit the audience, situation, and purpose. |
| **Logic**<br><br>A logical case informs—but rarely motivates. | **Emotion**<br><br>An emotional appeal persuades. |
| **Distortion**<br><br>Hearing only what's said leaves many gaps in one's understanding. | **Perspective**<br><br>Empathy, silence, understanding different points of view and cultures, and reading between the lines about what's not said often reveal the real message and produce the best outcome for negotiators. |

# Next Steps

If you'd like to go deeper on the subject, visit WhatMoreCanISay thebook.com, where you'll find resources and a PDF downloadable overview of the nine laws presented in this book.

# Acknowledgments

As with each book that has gone before, writing is rarely a solo effort. My work always builds on decades of prior research by teams of dedicated psychologists and social scientists, consulting assignments and cooperation by client organizations, and hours of personal interviews with clients willing to share their experiences and expertise.

I especially would like to thank the following individuals interviewed and quoted specifically within the pages here:

Tom Hund, executive vice president and CFO, BNSF Railway

David Parsley, senior vice president, Supply Chain Management, Brinker International

Catherine Hernandez-Blades, chief marketing and communications officer, Flextronics International, USA

Han Kieftenbeld, global chief procurement officer, Ingredion

Cheryl A. Barruso, senior vice president, PNC Bank, NA

Bob Danzig, former president, Hearst Newspapers

Jane Binger, EdD, RN, senior research officer, the Sutter Health Network

Also I would like to thank Jeanette Shaw at Penguin Random House for her vision for the book and keen editing eye. Particularly, it was once again wonderful to work with my agent, Carol Mann, and her team to help me select the right publishing house for this book.

My appreciation also goes to George Hendley, who read the manuscript in final stages and offered helpful feedback. Also a big thank-you to my husband, Vernon Rae, for feedback on the manuscript and help in collecting research.

# Resources

## By Dianna Booher and Booher Consultants

### Books: Selected Titles

*Creating Executive Presence: Look, Talk, Think, and Act Like a Leader*

*Communicate With Confidence: How to Say It Right the First Time and Every Time* (Revised and Expanded Edition)

*The Voice of Authority: 10 Communication Strategies Every Leader Needs to Know*

*Booher's Rules of Business Grammar: 101 Fast and Easy Ways to Correct the Most Common Errors*

*Your Signature Work: Creating Excellence and Influencing Others at Work*

*Your Signature Life: Pursuing God's Best Every Day*

*From Contact to Contract: 496 Proven Sales Tips to Generate More Leads, Close More Deals, Exceed Your Goals, and Make More Money*

*Speak With Confidence: Powerful Presentations That Inform, Inspire, and Persuade*

*E-Writing: 21st Century Tools for Effective Communication*

*Fresh-Cut Flowers for a Friend*

*The Little Book of Big Questions: Answers to Life's Perplexing Questions*

*Good Grief, Good Grammar*

*To the Letter: A Handbook of Model Letters for the Busy Executive*

*Great Personal Letters for Busy People*

*The Complete Letter Writer's Almanac*

*Clean Up Your Act: Effective Ways to Organize Paperwork and Get It Out of Your Life*

*Executive's Portfolio of Model Speeches for All Occasions*

*The New Secretary: How to Handle People as Well as You Handle Paper*

*Writing for Technical Professionals*

*Winning Sales Letters*

*Get a Life Without Sacrificing Your Career*

*Ten Smart Moves for Women*

*Get Ahead, Stay Ahead*

*The Worth of a Woman's Words*

*Well Connected: Power Your Own Soul by Plugging Into Others*

*Mother's Gifts to Me*

*The Esther Effect*

*Love Notes: From My Heart to Yours*

*First Thing Monday Morning*

## Workshops: Selected List

*Presentations That Work*

*Strategic Writing*

*Email Matters*

*Technical Writing*

*Developing Winning Proposals*

*Good Grief, Good Grammar*

*Communicate With Confidence*

*eService Communications*

*Customer Service Communications*

*Listening Until You Really Hear*

*Resolving Conflict Without Punching Someone Out*

*Meetings: Leading and Participating Productively*

*Negotiating So That Everyone Wins*

## For More Information on Training

Booher Consultants, LLC
817-318-6000
clients@booher.com
Booher.com
eStore: BooherDirect.com

## For More Information on Speaking or Executive Coaching

Booher Research Institute
817-283-2333
BooherResearch.com
clients@BooherResearch.com
@DiannaBooher
LinkedIn.com/In/DiannaBooher
Facebook.com/DiannaBooher
Plus.Google.com/DiannaBooher
YouTube.com/DiannaBooher
Pinterest.com/DiannaBooher

# Notes

## It's Not What You Think

1. Leo Widrich, "The Science of New Year's Resolutions: Why 88% Fail and How to Make Them Work," January 1, 2013, huliq.com/12092/new-years-resolutions-dont-last-long-survey-finds.

## Chapter 1: The Law of Trust vs. Distrust

1. Linda L. Price and Lawrence F. Feick, "The Role of Interpersonal Sources in External Search: An Informational Perspective," in *Advances in Consumer Research*, vol. 11, ed. Thomas C. Kinnear (Provo, UT: Association for Consumer Research), 250–55.

2. John Bussey, "A CEO Quits to Spend Time with Family—Really," *Wall Street Journal*, October 4, 2013.

3. Eddy Elmer and Greg Houran, "Physical Attractiveness in the Workplace," *Hotel News Resource*, 2008, hotelnewsresource.com/article31439.html; Anne Case and Christina Paxson, "Stature and Status: Height, Ability, and Labor Market Outcomes," *Journal of Political Economy* 116 (3) (2008), 499–532; Shelly Chaiken, "Communicator Physical Attractiveness and Persuasion," *Journal of Personality and Social Psychology* 37 (8) (1979), 1387–97.

4. Karen Dion, Ellen Berscheid, and Elaine Walster, "What Is Beautiful Is Good," *Journal of Personality and Social Psychology* 24 (1972), 285–90; Comila

Shahani-Denning, Purvi Dudhat, Roni Tevet, and Nicole Andreoli, "Effect of Physical Attractiveness on Selection Decisions in India and the United States," *International Journal of Management* 27 (1) (April 2010); Erin Shinners, "Effects of the 'What Is Beautiful Is Good' Stereotype on Perceived Trustworthiness," *University of Wisconsin–La Crosse Journal of Undergraduate Research* 12 (2009).

5. Sean Salter, Franklin G. Mixon Jr., and Ernest W. King, "Broker Beauty and Boon: A Study of Physical Attractiveness and Its Effect on Real Estate Brokers' Income and Productivity," *Applied Financial Economics* 22 (10) (May 2012), 811–25.

## Chapter 2: The Law of Collaboration vs. Monologue

1. Gretchen Gavett, "10 Charts from 2013 That Changed the Way We Think," HBR Blog Network, hbrblogs.files.wordpress.com/2013/12/10-charts-from-2013-that-changed-the-way-we-think/.

2. Kimberly D. Elsbach, "How to Pitch a Brilliant Idea," *Harvard Business Review* 81 (9) (September 2003), 117–23.

3. Robert B. Cialdini, *Influence: The Psychology of Persuasion* (New York: Harper-Collins, 2007).

4. Robin T. Peterson and Yam Limbu, "The Convergence of Mirroring and Empathy: Communications Training in Business-to-Business Personal Selling Persuasion Efforts," *Journal of Business-to-Business Marketing* 16 (3) (2009), 193–219; Christof Kuhbanderner, Reinhard Pekrun, and Markus A. Maier, "The Role of Positive and Negative Affect in the 'Mirroring' of Other Persons' Actions," *Cognitions & Emotion* 24 (7) (November 2010), 1182–90. Robin J. Tanner, Rosellina Ferraro, Tanya L. Chartrand, James R. Bettman, and Rick Van Baaren, "Of Chameleons and Consumption: The Impact of Mimicry on Choice and Preferences," *Journal of Consumer Research* 34 (6) (April 2008), 754–66.

5. Robin K. Dreeke and Joe Navarro, "Behavioral Mirroring in Interviewing," *FBI Law Enforcement Bulletin* 78 (12) (December 2009), 1–10.

6. Alberto Gallace and Charles Spence, "The Science of Interpersonal Touch: An Overview," *Neuroscience and Biobehavioral Reviews* 34 (2) (February 2010), 246–59. See the extensive bibliography listed within this article for research studies related to the topic of interpersonal touch as it relates to influencing people's behaviors.

7. David Blane and Stewart Mercer, "Compassionate Healthcare: Is Empathy the Key?" *Journal of Holistic Healthcare* 8 (3) (December 2011), 18–21.

8. Irene Etzkorn and Alan Siegel, *Simple: Conquering the Crisis of Complexity* (New York: Hachette/Twelve, 2013); Orville J. Messenger, "The Patient's Perception of Care: A Factor in Medical Litigation," *Canadian Family Physician* 35 (January l989). Findings from a research study by a U.S. physician-insurance group suggest that the single most frequent reason for lawsuits against physicians and hospitals was patients' perceptions of lack of concern or compassion—not medical mistakes. In a survey of 2,500 physicians, they themselves confirmed these findings in what would be their primary recommendation as the best deterrents to litigation: good communication and rapport with patients. Kristin E. Schleiter, "Difficult Patient-Physician Relationships and the Risk of Medical Malpractice Litigation," virtual mentor.ama-assn.org/2009/03/hlaw1-0903.html.

9. Stefano Del Canale, Daniel Z. Louis, Vittorio Maio, Xiaohong Wang, Giuseppina Rossi, Mohammadreza Hojat, Joseph S. Gonnella, "The Relationship Between Physician Empathy and Disease Complications: An Empirical Study of Primary Care Physicians and Their Diabetic Patients in Parma, Italy," *Academic Medicine* 87 (9) (September 2012).

## Chapter 3: The Law of Simplicity vs. Complexity

1. 42 West ad agency, *New York Times*, October 22, 2013.

2. Laura Landro, "The Talking Cure for Health Care: Improving the Ways Doctors Communicate with Their Patients Can Lead to Better Care—and Lower Costs," *Journal Reports: Health Care*, April 8, 2013. (She cites as her sources *Medical Care*; analysis by Texas State University and University of California, Riverside.)

3. Sarah Perez, "Twitpitch: The Elevator Pitch Hits Twitter," readwrite.com/2008/04/18.

4. Sheena S. Iyengar and Mark R. Lepper, "When Choice Is Demotivating: Can One Desire Too Much of a Good Thing?" *Journal of Personality and Social Psychology* 79 (6) (December 2000), 995–1006.

5. Bruce Horovitz, "Marketers Such as Starbucks Discover That Simple Sells," USAToday.com/money/industries/food/2009-10-27-marketers-simple-sell.

6. Lauren Weber, "Help Wanted—On Writing Job Descriptions," *Wall Street Journal*, October 2, 2013.

7. David Ogilvy, *Ogilvy on Advertising* (New York: Vintage Books, 1985); ogilvy .com/About/Our-History/Ogilvy_Mather.aspx.

8. Hyunjin Song and Norbert Schwarz. "If It's Hard to Read, It's Hard to Do: Processing Fluency Affects Effort Prediction and Motivation," *Psychological Science* (Wiley-Blackwell) 19 (10) (October 2008), 986–88.

9. Maria Veloso, *Web Copy That Sells: The Revolutionary Formula for Creating Killer Copy That Grabs Their Attention and Compels Them to Buy* (Third Edition). New York: AMACOM/American Management Association, 2013.

## Chapter 4: The Law of Tact vs. Insensitivity

1. Gregory Ciotti, copyblogger.com/persuasive-copywriting-words, June 19, 2013.

2. Roger Dooley, *Brainfluence: 100 Ways to Persuade and Convince Consumers with Neuromarketing* (Hoboken, NJ: John Wiley & Sons, 2012); Jason Zweig, *Your Money and Your Brain: How the New Science of Neuroeconomics Can Help Make You Rich* (New York: Free Press, 2007).

3. Ronald M. Shapiro and Jeff Barker, *Perfecting Your Pitch: How to Succeed in Business and Life* (New York: Hudson Street Press, 2013).

## Chapter 5: The Law of Potential vs. Achievement

1. Zakary L. Tormala, Jayson S. Jia, Michael I. Norton, "The Preference for Potential," *Journal of Personality and Social Psychology* 103 (4) (2012), 567–83.

2. Ibid., 568. The authors cite four previous studies from 2007 to 2010 on consumer behavior.

## Chapter 6: The Law of Distinction vs. Dilution

1. Kimberlee Weaver, Stephen M. Garcia, and Norbert Schwarz, "The Presenter's Paradox," *Journal of Consumer Research* 39 (3) (October 2012), 445–60.

2. Aaron R. Brough and Alexander Chernev, "When Opposites Detract: Categorical Reasoning and Subtractive Valuations of Product Combinations," *Journal of Consumer Research* 39 (2) (August 2012), 399–414.

## Chapter 7: The Law of Specificity vs. Generalization

1. Robert B. Cialdini, *Influence: The Psychology of Persuasion* (New York: Harper-Collins, 2007).
2. Randy Garner, "Post-It Note Persuasion: A Sticky Influence," *Journal of Consumer Psychology* 15 (3) (2005), 230–37.
3. Chris Janiszewski and Dan Uy, "Precision of the Anchor Influences the Amount of Adjustment," *Psychological Science* 19 (2) (February 2008), 121–27.
4. Sybil S. Yang, Sheryl E. Kimes, and Mauro M. Sessarego, "$ or Dollars: Effects of Menu-Price Formats on Restaurant Checks," *Cornell Hospitality Report* 9 (8) (May 2009).
5. Sarah Kershaw, "Using Menu Psychology to Entice Diners," *New York Times*, December 22, 2009.
6. Nicolas Gueguen and Celine Jacob, "Congruency Between Instrumental Background Music and Behavior on a Website," *Psychology of Music* 42 (1) (January 2014), 29–34, pom.sagepub.com/content/42/1/29.short.
7. Roger Dooley, *Brainfluence: 100 Ways to Persuade and Convince Consumers with Neuromarketing* (Hoboken, NJ: John Wiley & Sons, 2012), 35, 44–45, 88, 117–20.

## Chapter 8: The Law of Emotion vs. Logic

1. John Kotter and Dan Cohen, *The Heart of Change: Real-Life Stories of How People Change Their Organizations* (Boston: Harvard Business Review Press Books/Harvard Publishing, 2012).
2. Teppo Jarvinen, Raine Sihvonen, Mika Paavola, Antti Malmivaara, Ari Itala, Antti Joukainen, Heikki Nurmi, and Juha Kalske, "Arthroscopic Partial Meniscectomy versus Sham Surgery for a Degenerative Meniscal Tear," *New England Journal of Medicine* 369 (December 26, 2013), 2515–24.
3. Shaul Fox, "The Power of Emotional Appeals in Promoting Organizational Change Programs," *Academy of Management Executive* 15 (4) (November 2001), 84–94.
4. Sean Stannard-Stockton, "Making Charitable Appeals to Donors' Hearts and Heads," *Chronicle of Philanthropy* 22 (4) (November 26, 2009), 50.
5. Kenneth D. Chestek, "Judging by the Numbers: An Empirical Study of the Power of Story," *Journal of the Association of Legal Writing Directors* 7 (Fall 2010), 1–35.

6. Irith Hadas-Halpern and David Raveh, "Patient Photos Spur Radiologists' Empathy and Eye for Detail," Radiological Society of North America, press release, December 2, 2008.

7. Aradhna Krishna, May O. Lwin, and Maureen Morrin, "Product Scent and Memory," *Journal of Consumer Research* 37 (1) (June 2010), 57–67, jstor.org/stable /10/101086/649909.

## Chapter 9: The Law of Perspective vs. Distortion

1. Adam D. Galinsky, William W. Maddux, Debra Gilin, and Judith B. White, "Why It Pays to Get Inside the Head of Your Opponent: The Differential Effects of Perspective Taking and Empathy in Negotiations," *Psychological Science* 10 (4) (April 2008), 378–84.

# About the Author

**Dianna Booher**'s life work has centered around communication in all its forms: oral, written, interpersonal, and enterprise-wide. As author of forty-six books, translated into twenty-six languages, she has traveled the globe, talking with clients and organizations on six continents about communication challenges they face at work and at home. Despite the cultural differences, two things remain the same: Communication is the basic business act. And communication either cements or destroys personal and work relationships.

Improving communication skills, habits, and attitudes dramatically changes life—for an individual, a family, an organization, and a nation. Dianna considers that an exciting and rewarding goal for the communication training firm she founded in 1980, Booher Consultants Inc., as well as her newest company, Booher Research Institute.

Based in the Dallas–Fort Worth Metroplex, **Booher Consultants, LLC,** provides communication coaching, training, and consulting to some of the largest Fortune 500 companies and governmental agencies, among them: IBM, Lockheed Martin, BP, Chevron, ConocoPhillips, BNSF Railway, Ericsson, Alcatel-Lucent, Brinker International, Northwestern

Mutual, PepsiCo, Novartis, Bayer, the US Department of Veterans Affairs, and the US Naval Surface Warfare Center.

*Successful Meetings* magazine has named Dianna to its list of "21 Top Speakers for the 21st Century." The National Speakers Association has awarded her its highest honor: induction into the CPAE Speaker Hall of Fame.

The national media frequently interview Dianna for opinions on critical communication issues, including *Good Morning America*, *USA Today*, Fox, CNN, CNBC, Bloomberg, *Fortune*, *Forbes*, *Investor's Business Daily*, NPR, the *New York Times*, and the *Washington Post*. She holds a master's degree from the University of Houston.

For more information about training programs offered by Booher Consultants, visit booher.com.

For more information about Dianna's work and her speaking engagements, visit BooherResearch.com.